Growth on the Path

Based on
The Life and Oral Teachings of
Dr. Gayle C. Pierce

Cornelia Hoppe

A Handbook of Spiritual Tools
to Unleash the Power
Within You
as You Pursue
Your Individual Quest

Dr. Pierce, being universal in thought,
claimed no tradition as her own.

Book Design by Falcon Books

San Ramon, California

Order this book online at www.trafford.com/05-1527
or email orders@trafford.com

Most Trafford titles are also available at major online book retailers.

© Copyright 2008 Cornelia Hoppe.
All rights reserved. No part of this publication may be reproduced, stored in a retrieval system, or transmitted, in any form or by any means, electronic, mechanical, photocopying, recording, or otherwise, without the written prior permission of the author.

Note for Librarians: A cataloguing record for this book is available from Library and Archives Canada at www.collectionscanada.ca/amicus/index-e.html

Printed in Victoria, BC, Canada.

ISBN: 978-1-4120-6616-7

We at Trafford believe that it is the responsibility of us all, as both individuals and corporations, to make choices that are environmentally and socially sound. You, in turn, are supporting this responsible conduct each time you purchase a Trafford book, or make use of our publishing services. To find out how you are helping, please visit www.trafford.com/responsiblepublishing.html

Our mission is to efficiently provide the world's finest, most comprehensive book publishing service, enabling every author to experience success. To find out how to publish your book, your way, and have it available worldwide, visit us online at www.trafford.com/10510

 www.trafford.com

North America & international
toll-free: 1 888 232 4444 (USA & Canada)
phone: 250 383 6864 ♦ fax: 250 383 6804 ♦ email: info@trafford.com

The United Kingdom & Europe
phone: +44 (0)1865 487 395 ♦ local rate: 0845 230 9601
facsimile: +44 (0)1865 481 507 ♦ email: info.uk@trafford.com

10 9 8 7 6 5 4

THE GATEKEEPER

"Gatekeeper, tell me, why
are you closing this door?
What are you guarding so staunchly?"
"I am guarding the secret of quietude."
"But quietude is empty. Reliable people
say there is nothing in it."
"I know the secret of quietude.
I am placed to guard it."
"But your quietude is empty!"
"It is empty to you,"
replied the gatekeeper.

—Nicholas Roerich

The gate or door image serves as a metaphor for a spiritual threshold that the novice is searching for, without yet understanding the signs that are being revealed.

Growth on the Path is about Dr. Pierce's journey, my journey, and the journey of those who seek to understand and grow spiritually. It is about learning to live and love, overcoming challenges, changing one's self, learning truth, developing beingness, and honoring the self on both a spiritual and personal level.

—Cornelia Hoppe

Dedication

Growth on The Path is lovingly dedicated to Dr. Gayle C. Pierce, her friends, her students, her colleagues, and those whom she may have touched in her lifetime.

In fulfilling Dr. Pierce's spiritual mission as a teacher, a doctor, and a human being, this book is dedicated to the path of service, perception, awareness, and expanded God Consciousness.

Finally, it is dedicated to those who seek to learn, that they may find support for themselves on their journey.

Acknowledgments

Heartfelt thanks to Daniel Entin, Director of the Nicholas Roerich Museum, for permission to reprint the works of Nicholas Roerich.

To Vivian McCullough who, at the request of Dr. Pierce, supported and guided the weekly training sessions during Dr. Pierce's absence in Japan;

To Dorothy Kani for her contributions to the reading and organization of these teachings;

To Kathy Sullivan for her pertinent comments in the initial editing of this book;

To Patrick Tribble D.C., who provided insights into the teachings of Dr. Pierce; without these perceptions and collaboration with editing, I feel this book would not be complete;

To Robin and Terrill Keeler who offered several years of personal letters and notes from Dr. Pierce's group;

To Neil Christopherson, who supported the further editing, formatting, and publishing of this book;

To Rose Marie Wolf who, near the completion of this book, offered extensive time, direction and insight to clarify and simplify the material;

To Diana Ariza-Klose, for her ability, efficiency and perception in refining the material and formatting it on the computer;

And I thank all those who provided input and support toward the creation of this book.

Foreword

Shortly before Dr. Pierce's transition, I asked her if she wished to put into print the training and development sessions that I had taped some years before. She nodded affirmatively. I believe that these materials have a specific purpose to help those who seek to expand their consciousness and increase their awareness. I have sought to create a legacy of Dr. Pierce's teachings that others can learn from and practice on their spiritual journey.

Dr. Pierce often said, "All paths lead to God." She honored all traditions and religions. She encouraged others to deepen their spiritual connection to God. In reading this book, particularly the materials involving healing, you may wish to chant, vocalize a mantra, or offer a prayer that is more in alignment with your beliefs than the prayers used by Dr. Pierce and her students.

All spoken information in this book, including dialogue, was taken word for word from a tape machine, to a typewriter, then to a computer, and finally to these pages. Brackets and notes in the text have been added where clarification seemed necessary.

May the light shine for you and give you knowledge and understanding throw out the years my love
to Gayle

Dr. Gayle C. Pierce
August 20, 1903 - March 15, 1999

The Buddha
A painting by Elizabeth Brunner
Presented to Dr. Gayle C. Pierce by the artist

Contents

ILLUSTRATIONS	17
INTRODUCTION	19
DR. PIERCE	19
Teacher	19
Healer	22
Seeker	26
I. QUOTATIONS FROM DR. PIERCE	37
II. THE USE OF LIGHT AND POWER	67
Individual Healings	67
Emergency Power	70
Obstructions	70
III. METHODS OF PROTECTION	75
Prayer	78
Cleansing	80
IV. RELEASING AND CUTTING CORDS	87
V. PRAYER AND MEDITATION	99
VI. THE AURIC FIELD	111
Aura	111
Psychic Attack	119
VII. HEALING	123

VIII. TRANSITION	137
IX. ANGELS	147
X. COLOR	151
XI. REMINISCENCES OF OGAMISAMA	155
XII. OM MANI PADMA HUM	163
XIII. AGNI YOGA	165
Definition	165
Terms	167
XIV. INFLUENTIAL PEOPLE	171
Elizabeth Brunner	171
His Holiness the Fourteenth Dalai Lama	174
Max Heindel	176
Helena Shaposhnikova Roerich	179
Nicholas Roerich	181
Ogamisama	184
RECOLLECTIONS	188
FROM THE AUTHOR	193
BOOK LIST	197

Illustrations

1. The Gatekeeper—Nicholas Roerich 5
2. Personal Message from Dr. Pierce 12
3. Dr. Gayle C. Pierce 13
4. The Buddha, Painting by Elizabeth Brunner 14
5. The Venerable Geshe Ngawang Dhargyey 30
6. The Venerable Geshe Larampa Rabten Rinpoche . . . 31
7. Dr. Pierce—India 1960s 43
8. Building Dedicated to Dr. Pierce 97
9. Ogamisama, Tabuse, Yamaguchi Pref. Japan 1967 . . 161
10. Elizabeth Brunner—New Delhi, India 1997 173
11. Dr. Pierce and the Dalai Lama, Tibetan
    New Year's Day—Dharamsala, India 1986 175
12. Max Heindel 178
13. Helena Roerich—1937 180
14. Banner of Peace designed by Nicholas Roerich 182
15. Nicholas Roerich—United States, 1934 183
16. Ogamisama, Tabuse, Yamaguchi Pref. Japan, 1967 . . 186
17. Ogamisama with Dr. Pierce, Tabuse, Yamaguchi Pref.
    Japan, 1965. 187

INTRODUCTION

Fanny Gail Coombs was born in Idaho in 1903 to a Mormon sheep-herding family. Early in life, she replaced her first name with her middle name and altered the spelling of Gail to Gayle. When she married, her surname changed from Coombs to Pierce. Dr. Pierce or "Dr. Gayle" as she was called, initially practiced as a nurse and an anesthetist for ten years. On February 19, 1938, she was licensed as a chiropractor and naturopathic physician.

DR. PIERCE—TEACHER

Dr. Pierce demonstrated a particular ability to be involved with and concerned for each human being. Because of her continuous support, encouragement, and acknowledgment, each person, whether student or patient, had the opportunity to develop a greater sense of self-confidence, a sense of honor, and a purposeful dedication to a personal spiritual path. She introduced people to Light, to a higher Universal Consciousness, and to the quest for understanding and spiritual fulfillment.

Dr. Pierce taught of the universal principle of Light that dwells within us. This teaching resulted in the student's having an increased awareness of Universal Consciousness, another term for God or Light. She spoke of God Consciousness, Universal Light, and the Universal Presence. Dr. Pierce, a fervent seeker on her path, guided others to be seekers on their paths as well. She often said, "Work with what you have."

A major building block for Dr. Pierce's spiritual foundation was Agni Yoga, which teaches that the evolution of planetary consciousness is of utmost importance and that the individual through spiritual striving can attain this consciousness. Agni Yoga teaches a spiritual path of practice for daily life.

Dr. Pierce, because she was influenced by Agni Yoga, worked with Light to remove those obstacles that cause spiritual disturbances. She perceived a person's needs and knew how to work with them. She had the ability to assist those who were embroiled in negative experiences, those who were assaulted with curses or psychic attacks, and those who were dying or who had passed over (i.e., in transition). Because of her knowledge, many people who were prayed for were cleansed of negativity, purified, and released.

She utilized and directed Light to discharge thought forms called elementals which can be harmful to an individual. A person, who over a long period of time, has repeatedly held the same negative or positive thoughts, creates these forms.

Dr. Pierce also spoke of the necessity of strengthening the will in order to progress on the path and to cope with the challenges encountered. Her teachings of the use of Light, methods of personal protection, the cutting of cords for releasing ties which bind individuals, the clearing of impingements in the aura, and her medical knowledge of health blockages, along with intuition and awareness, were essential tools for healing.

During the 1960s and 1970s when recreational drug use was popular, people indiscriminately delved into spiritual practices beyond their understanding. This often resulted in health and mental disorders. Dr. Pierce assisted them in cleansing their auras to regain physical and emotional stability. She did not absorb negative energy from the person or situation because of her knowledge of the practice of Light and the *power of protection*. Because of her knowledge and her use of the divine quality of Light, seeds of understanding were planted in these individuals. In time they began to acquire discrimination in the practice and use of Light, to experience and affirm it, and to realize that they were a part of the Universal or Divine Consciousness.

She frequently received prayer requests from individuals, or from family members concerning the transmuting of family or business problems, or requests for the removal of obstacles that interfered with someone's well-being. Dr. Pierce stressed that prayer work must be in accord with the will of the individual being prayed for and must be for his or her highest good. She also stated that any person who prays for another must remain objective in order not to take on the person's emotions or problems as this would involve taking on the karma of the person being prayed for.

Dr. Pierce's selflessness and dedication to the path of service served as an example to others and was significant in inspiring those who quested for spiritual knowledge.

DR. PIERCE—HEALER

Dr. Pierce, an early proponent and practitioner of radionics, owned an Electro Biometer, a radionic instrument designed and built by Thomas Galen Hieronymus (1895-1988). This device measures the energetic disorganization of the organism to the extent that it deviates from the norm. She utilized this instrument to obtain readings that measured the patient's vitality and aura. This enabled her to diagnose and treat diseases not yet manifested on the physical plane. She also used radionics to implement a brain radiation technique that measured a person's soul quality. This specific knowledge enabled her to teach at the level of a person's spiritual capacity, which frequently resulted in the acceleration of his or her spiritual advancement.

Because the FDA allowed the radionic device to be used only for treating crops, Dr. Pierce's machine bore a protective sign "For Research Only."

She taught that disease begins in the etheric body, the energetic blueprint of the physical body, six to twelve months before it manifests on the physical plane. She said that it is possible to heal sickness before it appears on the physical plane by focusing radionic treatment on the etheric body, also known as the etheric double. When treating the physical ailments of the patient, it was often necessary to focus on both the physical plane and the etheric level. Though she was able to discover disease before physical manifestation, there were cases where Dr. Pierce recognized that a terminal disease could not be treated because of karmic causes.

Her ability to speak to patients regarding their ongoing issues, their relationships, and sometimes the link of their current experiences to their childhood as well as to previous reincarnations was remarkable. Her capacity to understand, to communicate with ease, and to converse with others went beyond religious and philosophical bases. Her nursing and chiropractic education also served as an avenue for healing.

An important component of Dr. Pierce's healing art was cranial therapy, a technique developed by the osteopaths Terence J. Bennett and William G. Sutherland. This specialized therapy was designed to work with the muscles, bones, and sutures of the skull in order to release any toxins and tensions held in these areas. Through the release of embedded toxins, this procedure enabled the person's consciousness to be lifted, his vibrations raised, and allowed for the general improvement of his health. With the implementation of cranial therapy, spiritual development was usually accelerated. Patients receiving this treatment were few in number, because they had to have both the desire to receive this therapy and the tolerance to withstand the sharp pain and increased toxicity caused by the use of combs, forks, spoons, rocks, and metal pieces that were applied to the skull with firm pressure to effect change on the physical, mental, and spiritual planes.

People from many countries with various beliefs and cultural backgrounds traveled to consult with Dr. Pierce. Though most individuals came for chiropractic treatment, others came to discuss worldly or spiritual concerns or both. Neither belief nor religion was questioned. Whether Buddhist, Hindu, Christian, Jew, Muslim, agnostic, or atheist, Dr. Pierce spoke a common language to all. She provided a safe environment to discuss individual concerns, household issues, career matters, relationship worries, and spiritual development. Many who visited her did not initially understand the purpose of their meeting. In retrospect, they often said it was Divine Guidance coupled with fate that led them to her door. She was a doctor and healer; for others, a teacher and mentor, and for some, a colleague and friend.

Introduction

Dr. Pierce encouraged and fostered each person's finding of his spiritual path. She taught that the individual's striving was of utmost importance to develop spiritually. For people who believed in angels she spoke of angels, and she encouraged them to develop relationships with the angelic kingdom. With others, she spoke of the twelve Masters, particularly Moraya, Kuthumi, Babaji, Buddha, and Christ, whose missions are to teach the paths of knowledge, wisdom, and love, all of which are necessary for spiritual evolution. Dr. Pierce was also well-versed in the teachings of Theosophy, Agni Yoga, Gurdjieff, Ouspensky, Tibetan Buddhism, and Mystical Christianity. She had a particular reverential relationship with the Christ Consciousness.

She was not bound or limited by religious or philosophical traditions. Because she was universal in thought, she had connections with various beliefs including those of Native Americans. "Chiefy," Chief of the Tuolumne Tribe, was a close friend. Together they participated in sweat lodge ceremonies where healing Light was directed toward individuals, groups, cultures, and Mother Earth. She worked closely with the spirit guide Running Horse, as well as with other American Indian spirit guides.

Dr. Pierce attracted people like a beacon of light. It was astonishing to note the arrival of such a steady stream of international visitors who came to receive physical healing, spiritual fulfillment, and relaxation. Those who came often stayed for a day, a week, a month, or even as long as a year. Dr. Pierce was endowed with a spiritual awareness and an intellectual understanding of others.

Dr. Pierce dedicated herself to the study of many diverse traditions, teachings, and religions, but she was primarily devoted to the essence of a teaching, rather than its form.

DR. PIERCE—SEEKER

Dr. Pierce indicated that her spiritual path began at the age of 55. She studied Theosophy, attended a Dianetics group in Palo Alto, and in 1954, a large group led by Ralph Harris Houston held its meetings in her home in San Jose, California. Ralph Houston, known as Guru RHH, was a disciple of Nicholas Roerich. He was the only Western Guru to teach Agni Yoga, which he taught from 1942 until his death in 1976. Each year, while studying with Guru RHH, the group went to Mount Shasta, California for a retreat. On one auspicious occasion when Dr. Pierce was hiking with the group in Mount Shasta, a voice from the wilderness called her name. She went to the spot where she heard the voice. She was instructed that Christ, rather than Buddha, was her primary teacher. With reverence, she then aligned herself with the Christ Consciousness and the esoteric teachings of the Mystical Christ Consciousness. After her experience in the wilderness, Dr. Pierce started a metaphysical study group in her home that focused on reincarnation and its connection to the energies carried over by the individual from his past lives. This group's focus later shifted to Agni Yoga.

When this group disbanded in the mid 1970s, Dr. Pierce received a request from the children of these members to begin a spiritual study group that focused on the teachings of the *Psychological Commentaries on the Teaching of Gurdjieff and Ouspensky, Vols. 1-5*, by Maurice Nicoll. Later, Agni Yoga and methods of healing were studied in addition to various spiritual traditions and teachings. This group continued meeting in her home until 1997.

Dr. Pierce reached out in many directions for her studies; she integrated teachings from many philosophies. She read voraciously and retained what she read. What she absorbed she articulated to others. Because of her intense commitment to her spiritual development and because of her continued dedication to the growth and healing of others, these strivings merited her many gifts of the Spirit which included perception, understanding, creativity, and healing. For a long time she had the gifts of perception and instant knowing of what was needed when she greeted a patient or an individual in need. Years later Dr. Pierce stated that she had not respected these gifts enough, because as she aged this perception and instant knowing diminished.

In the 1960s, Dr. Pierce traveled to Japan several times to be with Ogamisama, a spiritual teacher whom she had met in Palo Alto, California, in 1965. She worried about the length of time she would be away from her patients. Ogamisama told her not to be concerned, that she needed to be in Japan, and upon her return to the United States she would have an even greater practice. She stayed for three months, and her practice grew as Ogamisama had predicted.

Dr. Pierce stated many times that she would not have a teacher in this lifetime; however, Ogamisama, who transmitted power to her, was an influential teacher. Dr. Pierce visited Honbu, the headquarters of Ogamisama's temple in Tabuse, Japan eight times. She became Ogamisama's personal physician. When Ogamisama was seriously ill, only Dr. Pierce was allowed to touch her. As always, Dr. Pierce traveled with a portable radionics instrument.

From the mid 1960s until 1986, Dr. Pierce made several trips to India, where she met many Tibetans, including the Dalai Lama. She became involved with their culture and sacred teachings. By the late 1960s, she had absorbed much of Tibetan Buddhism, the study of which she likened to "a glass of fresh water." She developed relationships and provided healthcare to the Tibetans and to the Tibetan teachers (lamas). She cultivated a special kinship with the Venerable Geshe Ngawang Dhargyey, the first Lama appointed by the Dalai Lama in 1971 to start a teaching program for Westerners at the Tibetan Library of Archives in Dharamsala, India. When Dr. Pierce attended Geshe Dhargyey's lectures she

Introduction

understood and received direct knowledge from his teachings, though she neither spoke nor understood Tibetan. She had a special friendship with the Venerable Geshe Larampa Rabten Rinpoche, the first Tibetan Master to give the dharma or religious teachings in Dharamsala in 1969 to Westerners. He was also the first Tibetan Master who gave teachings in the West in 1974.

Both of these highly respected Tibetan Lamas gave teachings at Dr. Pierce's home on several occasions. Whenever they visited Dr. Pierce, they received medical advice and treatment from her. Both Lamas were dedicated and involved in bringing Dharma (spiritual teachings) of the Mahayana tradition to Westerners. During two of Geshe Dhargyey's visits with Dr. Pierce, he gave the Medicine Buddha initiation to the members of her group.

Oil painting on glass was one of the many creative gifts she received as a result of her striving on the spiritual path. No form of study was necessary. The caliber of her work was such that a New York museum requested an exhibit. She demonstrated other creative abilities in rapid succession. The scope of these gifts helped to instill in people a desire to discover their inner creative potential. Dr. Pierce's vast amount of knowledge was instrumental in guiding and imparting to others a pursuit and dedication to spiritual growth.

Dr. Pierce possessed both a charismatic quality and a great fountain of knowledge that attracted people to her. Her

The Ven. Geshe Ngawang Dhargyey

The Ven. Geshe Larampa Rabten Rinpoche

dedication to the individual's deepening of spiritual growth and understanding through striving was of the utmost importance to her. The universal appeal of this approach was evidenced by the diversity of people who joined her groups, many of whom retained their religion or affiliation but absorbed the Universal Principles and deepened their spiritual dedication.

Dr. Pierce met with the Dalai Lama on numerous occasions, both in America and in India. At times they discussed the needs and the problems of the exiled Tibetan community. There is a story of a conversation between the Dalai Lama and Dr. Pierce regarding the exiled Tibetans' need for agricultural cattle since the sacred Indian cow was not available for use. Bringing cows in by boat was discussed. The Dalai Lama suddenly burst into laughter and he said "seasick cows." Because of the Dalai Lama's concern and compassion for the plight of the cows during their voyage by sea, the idea was abandoned.

The Dalai Lama had several tutors appointed to him in his early childhood, one of whom was the Junior Tutor who supervised his education and spiritual development. While Dr. Pierce was in Dharamsala, India, the Junior Tutor suffered a medical emergency. She informed him that he must go to the hospital immediately to have his gallbladder removed. Because of her intercession, his life was saved, and the Dalai Lama was forever grateful.

Introduction

A cherished friend in India was Rinchen Dolma Taring (Mary), the author of *Daughter of Tibet*, the first biography written in English by a Tibetan. In 1959 as the Chinese were invading Tibet, she watched a hail of bullets fly in front of her home in Lhasa but was unable to enter her home to rescue her children who fled at a later time. To decrease the likelihood of capture and possible execution of herself and her family, she chose to flee alone from Tibet by traversing the Himalayan Mountains into India. During Mary's plight, her husband Jigme, an official of the young Dalai Lama, fled separately with the Dalai Lama on a secret escape over the treacherous Himalayas. Because of their flight from Tibet, the Tarings lost all of their worldly possessions. Several months later, Mary and Jigme were reunited in India. They forsook their royal status and dedicated themselves to the path of service. At the Dalai Lama's request and under his direction, the Tarings opened schools for Tibetan refugee children. Mary also founded the Tibetan Homes Foundation in Dehradun, India to house displaced elderly Tibetans. Until the end of her life in 2002, at the age of 92, she worked tirelessly to raise funds for Tibetans, especially for the care of the elderly. Dr. Pierce, because of her friendship with the Tarings, the Dalai Lama, and other Tibetans, formed a foundation to provide financial support to several Tibetan projects including the Tibetan Homes Foundation, the office of the Dalai Lama, and a nunnery in Dharamsala for Western and Tibetan nuns.

The Taring's home was in Dehradun, an Indian hill station known as Uttarakhand or "Land of the Gods" which is 230 kilometers from New Delhi. While visiting them, Dr. Pierce saw and admired many paintings by Nicholas Roerich, whose residence was not far from Mary and Jigme's home.

Another influential friend in Dr. Pierce's life was the artist Elizabeth Brunner, who was born in Hungary. Elizabeth and her mother Elizabeth Sass Brunner, also an artist, traveled together in their search for spiritual understanding. While in Italy, Elizabeth Brunner dreamed of a male figure. She related her dream to her mother who identified the image as the Indian poet Rabindranath Tagore. Elizabeth then wrote a letter to Tagore, who invited them both to visit him in India. In 1930, they made India their home. Both Elizabeth and her mother's paintings served as a bridge between Europe and India. Jawaharlal Nehru, Prime Minister of India, bestowed upon Elizabeth an award for her contribution to Indian culture.

Elizabeth presented a painting of the Buddha to Dr. Pierce as a token of gratitude and friendship. This painting was displayed on the wall of Dr. Pierce's living room in San Jose, California. As she led groups it was a focus of reverence. The presence of the Buddha was felt by many.

DR. PIERCE—TRANSITION

When Dr. Pierce encountered health problems, she did not use them as obstacles to prevent her from aiding those who sought her help.

Her initial health difficulty occurred when she hastened to answer a telephone and slipped on a wet floor, fracturing several vertebrae. A year or two later, while watering her plants early one morning in 1981, she tripped over a garden hose and broke her hip. Although the hip replacement was successful, the bonding material did not adhere to the bone. Because of this, she endured constant pain. She also experienced several strokes. The first occurred in 1991, and inhibited her speech and writing ability. Because of a strong determination and intensive therapy, Dr. Pierce recovered most of her speaking ability and some of her writing skills. Within a year, she was once again treating patients. Despite her diminished physical capacity she continued to work with intense dedication and service. A few years later a second stroke permanently limited her speech. She neither complained nor spoke of these trials. Dr. Pierce acknowledged the lesson of pain as a teacher and indicated that she was grateful for the challenge. Though in pain, she remained busy and active. When there was a reprieve, she loved to be in the garden working with her plants. With her health diminished by strokes, a weakened heart, and limited ability to communicate, it was indeed difficult for Dr. Pierce. She continued to treat patients as long as she was physically able. On March 15, 1999, conscious and aware, Dr. Pierce left this earthly plane.

Chapter I

QUOTATIONS FROM DR. PIERCE

"Time is an indefinite factor."

—Gayle C. Pierce

ANGER

"There is good and bad anger. There can be a constructive or righteous anger which is creative, but when anger is destructive, it tears down deeply and destroys. Bad anger is destructive to both the person who sends it and to the person who receives it. It affects others, but it is more destructive to the person who sends it than it is to the recipient.

"Anger can completely destroy a person. Righteous anger is controlled anger, and it is used for a reason or as a tool to achieve an end result. All emotions can be used as a tool, but a person has to know how to use the force. It is like a power saw. If someone misuses it, it could cut an arm off. It is the same thing with anger. It can cut part of a person off, but used with control, it is a powerful tool as any emotion is. Learn how to control anger, use it as a tool, and never let yourself get caught in it.

ASTROLOGY

"It is a higher organizational level above the personality. It is amazingly accurate and a good learning tool. Astrology is one of the ways of truth, and truth is at all levels. Accept the fact that there is a planetary influence on man both for good and for bad. Accept this and deal with it.

AWARENESS

"Spiritualism and spirituality are not the same thing. The growth of the Spirit will give you spiritual essence, and this is true spirituality. First of all, we have to have an awareness of our oneness with God and know the quality that is God, and know this deep desire for God and the presence of the Spirit. This is one of the awarenesses that we have to have first. Then we have to use the awareness.

"We know, for example, that just the 'word of mouth' does not help us, because awareness has to be a part of our daily living growth. It is like Ogamisama said: 'As you did your work, did you chant the *Na-myo-ho-ren-ge-kyos*?' In the back of my mind, it goes on all the time. It is not just the chant; it is doing the work with attention, but attention on God too.

"And in *Light on the Path*, it is written: 'Live not in the present or the past, but in the eternal.' This giant weed, which is ego, cannot grow there, but we have to be aware of the eternal, to be aware that God is the eternal, so I have to live in God and be conscious of this God part of us and aware that there is more within the heart. If you have love for humanity — the deep love for humanity or for God—this too is an expression of God, the awareness that there is something bigger than one's self and the emotions that must then come in are more than we know. This is very important and these are things that we must realize.

BIBLE

"The Bible is an Eastern book composed by Jews who never put anything lightly. It is written in parables with hidden meanings. There are parts that are so beautiful they sing.

BLOCKAGES

"We must always remain impersonal when doing the work. We bring in the White Light of Universal Consciousness all through the house, cleansing and purifying each person. Then we put on the 'Armor of Light.' The Light must be tempered according to that person's needs. We then bring in whatever is needed for the growth of the Spirit. Light and energy must be brought in through the top of the head and down through the spiritual centers in order to release blockages of negativity. Bringing energy up through the feet could block organs in the sacral region and solar plexus. This is why it is important to bring energy for healing in from the top of the head downward. Light flows through the sacral region, the solar plexus, and the central nervous system. These centers of the spine are like nerve centers. If you get blockages at these centers, you will have a hard time getting rid of them so that the spiritual energy can flow. This is why we have to be extremely careful and protective at all times of the spiritual centers located up and down the spine.

CHILDREN

"It takes a year to get used to a new baby, to get used to the adjusting and the constant needs or demands. We grow as our love grows. Children shake us out of ourselves.

CHRISTMAS

"The Light of Christ has touched some few men deeply to move them toward God and humanity. We pay homage to Him who is so little understood. At this time I reach out with the rose-red Light of Love, His symbol—the red rose—to all those who are close to me. I pick up my cross, His symbol, to bear it proudly and I hope well. I strive for purity of thought and action. I try to see as much of His Golden Light as I can see. All truth is one. All rays of light blend into white, which is the Light of the star that led to baby Jesus, the White Light of God, of understanding, of all knowledge and the power of good. I visualize the lily, the symbol of the path of the new man. For this Christmas, I send love and Light to you. I will see you in this Light on Christmas morning. I send you joy and success, for this too is yours.

CLEANSING

"The feet have so many reflexes in them. They are so vital and they are different in many ways. The Bible mentions the washing of the feet to cleanse them of negativity. This is also why we wash the hands. When a person sleeps, he becomes rested and relaxed. When the feet perspire, negativity or poison is being eliminated. This is why it is necessary to wash our feet often. After you have worked with anyone, you must wash your hands of any vibrations you have picked up.

"Water is the biggest cleanser we have. Going into the ocean takes out negative vibrations, as does bathing. Postulate when you are taking a shower, 'I am cleansing.' This affirmation goes to the subconscious, and you are therefore cleansing your body and the subconscious of anything negative. This is one of the Huna teachings of Hawaii. Every body organ has an interrelationship with the spiritual consciousness of the individual. There are many different levels, and the body is the tool that holds these levels and the Spirit together. When a person loses a hand or a foot, the counterpart, the etheric body, still has hands and feet. This is why healing and cleansing are done on the etheric body, the pattern from which the body is originally made. When working with someone, cleanse the auric field with the White Light. Then send the White Light through the body from the top of the head to the tips of the toes. The patient can also visualize the White Light within himself. Then send the Light in through the center of the forehead, sending it down neutralizing all negativity and sending healing to every cell in the body. Then bring the rose-red Light of Love into the heart center, sending it out with every beat of the heart to every cell of the body, revitalizing, restoring and giving whatever is necessary.

CREATIVE FORCE

"The sex force is a Creative Force called sex because of procreation, but this force is also used for creative energy. This same force can be used for creating a picture, for writing, for doing a flower arrangement, for teaching children, or for doing anything. This is the same force as a sex urge, but it is used in a different way. This force can be pulled up from the liver, the main center of gravity. We call this transmuting. Just as we can transmute negativity into something positive, we can transmute this power into this beautiful creative force of any kind we like. This is all the same power. This is the creative force of the body. This is why it is such an important vortex or center. We must transmute this energy and bring it into love or into the positive creative power of the Spirit.

knowledge and the power of good. I visualize the lily, the symbol of the path of the new man. For this Christmas, I send love and Light to you. I will see you in this Light on Christmas morning. I send you joy and success, for this too is yours.

CLEANSING

"The feet have so many reflexes in them. They are so vital and they are different in many ways. The Bible mentions the washing of the feet to cleanse them of negativity. This is also why we wash the hands. When a person sleeps, he becomes rested and relaxed. When the feet perspire, negativity or poison is being eliminated. This is why it is necessary to wash our feet often. After you have worked with anyone, you must wash your hands of any vibrations you have picked up.

"Water is the biggest cleanser we have. Going into the ocean takes out negative vibrations, as does bathing. Postulate when you are taking a shower, 'I am cleansing.' This affirmation goes to the subconscious, and you are therefore cleansing your body and the subconscious of anything negative. This is one of the Huna teachings of Hawaii. Every body organ has an interrelationship with the spiritual consciousness of the individual. There are many different levels, and the body is the tool that holds these levels and the Spirit together. When a person loses a hand or a foot, the counterpart, the etheric body, still has hands and feet. This is why healing and cleansing are done on the etheric body, the pattern from which the body is originally made. When working with someone, cleanse the auric field with the White Light. Then send the White Light through the body from the top of the head to the tips of the toes. The patient can also visualize the White Light within himself. Then send the Light in through the center of the forehead, sending it down neutralizing all negativity and sending healing to every cell in the body. Then bring the rose-red Light of Love into the heart center, sending it out with every beat of the heart to every cell of the body, revitalizing, restoring and giving whatever is necessary.

CREATIVE FORCE

"The sex force is a Creative Force called sex because of procreation, but this force is also used for creative energy. This same force can be used for creating a picture, for writing, for doing a flower arrangement, for teaching children, or for doing anything. This is the same force as a sex urge, but it is used in a different way. This force can be pulled up from the liver, the main center of gravity. We call this transmuting. Just as we can transmute negativity into something positive, we can transmute this power into this beautiful creative force of any kind we like. This is all the same power. This is the creative force of the body. This is why it is such an important vortex or center. We must transmute this energy and bring it into love or into the positive creative power of the Spirit.

"This power is transmuted by the mind, heart, or whatever center we bring it into, and it is then transmuted into whatever we wish to create. It is not the same as the force that creates anger.

DEATH

"As I get older it is there but not a menacing shadow, rather as part of my world. I know I will do what needs to be done. In addition, may I take what comes in, and in that, too, there is growth. I do not want too much, only enough to finish with dignity and strength what I need to do. Then to go, preferably very quickly, which is always a gift of the Spirit. I may even have a dividend of time. We must take care of the 'precious' body. I may live a hundred years, but only if the mind is clear. That is important, but concern, no. For if it comes it will be the time it should. And there is the life that follows, as surely as night follows day.

"Death is a part of life. You are young but all bodies are growing old. It will only be a matter of time. But remember, death is only a transition, a change. We must do what we can do in this lifetime in order to have a high evolution in another life. We must keep our awareness until the end. This is my reality.

DESIRE BODY

"I found a new thing about the Desire Body. It is ovoid in shape. It is like the aura, and all of the sides have vortexes. The desire body has a circumference of sixteen inches; two vortexes

Dr. Pierce
India, 1960s

above the head, one at the pelvis, one around the liver, and two around the knees. The power goes out from the liver vortex. It is all colors, and the colors are very vivid and very brilliant. Awareness increases in the individual who has awareness, though he may not know it. If he uses it in the wrong way, the energies go counterclockwise, but for the individual who uses the energy correctly, this energy goes clockwise and this energy is stronger.

"The Desire Body leaves us at night and goes into another state of consciousness to work out problems and other occurrences that have happened during the day. Sometimes this body tries to present these happenings back to us in the sleeping world. This is the part that leaves us in sleep for re-evaluation. As the individual becomes more aware, the energy of his Desire Body becomes brighter and more scintillating. This is what Max Heindel says.

"All bodies must be balanced. This Desire Body, which is one of the bodies that helps keep the balance, keeps the physical body in health and keeps the tissues where they belong. But in itself, it never takes any physical form. At death, the Desire Body leaves the physical body in a cloud form. On the other side, it takes a form in the same shape as the physical body at the time of death.

"The etheric double which is the Desire Body is also called the blueprint of the body or the vital body. It superimposes over the physical body. This substance which is all around the body has beautiful colors that are in movement all of the time. The physical body is like the yolk, and the Desire Body is like the white of the egg.

"When man stood up, the power went in through the vertebrae and the spinal cord and also down from the head. The vortex of power comes into us through the top of the head and goes downward through the body. The vortexes correspond somewhat to the chakras, but they are not quite the same. They are about six inches above the head, very alive with beautiful colors and have to do with balance and locomotion.

"The more aware we are, the more awareness we have and the stronger the vortex of power. The vortex is a vital, potent and stimulating power. The awareness increases the rays of power which may be seen as numerous colors generally unseen by us. These rays are in addition to the colors of the spectrum with which we are familiar.

"Orange, the basic color of the Desire Body is affected by how we feel. The basic reflection of color comes from the planet one is born under. With Mars, there is a pinkish cast to this color, and with Jupiter there is a pale blue cast.

"The basic colors scintillate and are in constant movement around us. You can see how it is if someone you do not like is around you and how you feel. This Desire Body may be what the aura is. The colors are brilliant and scintillating with constant movement going from one place to another, and they are very vital and alive. In the center of the movement is the vortex with pulls of different kinds that keep the Desire Body in constant motion. The liver is the main center of gravity. The vortexes keep going all the time. The smaller vortexes are at the knees, the larger ones at the liver and pelvis."

DISCRIMINATION, DISCERNMENT, WISDOM

Dr. Pierce taught that the student who is dedicated to the spiritual path must at some point earn the gifts of discrimination and discernment in order to further attain spiritual growth. She spoke of discrimination and discernment as gifts of the Spirit and wisdom as being a fruit of the Spirit. She reiterated this teaching countless times over the years.

"Discrimination is one of the first demands of the path of true discipleship; it is the discernment of actions, the causes of the actions, and the knowledge of which forces can harm and which forces can help the student on the path. Discernment implies keenness and discriminating accuracy. The disciple must strive consistently and persistently to discipline his own consciousness.

"As an individual strives on the spiritual path, and as he excels and increases his capacity by working with the circumstances that were given to him, this helps to advance the understanding and the awareness of spiritual tradition. The integration of these gifts at some point is mandatory for the understanding of spiritual teachings and for growth and advancement on the spiritual path.

Discrimination applies to every aspect of living and to every aspect of spiritual growth; thus the student is able to both discern and discriminate for himself what is the highest good for that moment in time. The Tibetans speak of this as *discriminating wisdom*.

DREAMS

"Try writing down your dreams. What they say comes from the Light within you.

EASTER

"At Easter time, we go forward toward a higher awareness of the beauty of the Christ, His Light that brings compassion, wisdom and healing. The new birth – it is in us. We bring the Light into the heart center letting it freely flow out into the rest of our being. Feel the new life force come in. Take in three deep breaths. Then exhale so deeply that it depresses the diaphragm. This is the letting out of the old. Now breathe in Light and love. Know that this breath is the reborn Christ in you. A new life! A new way! Feel the power coming into you. Make this time a new beginning. Know that within you is the life, love and Light, and try to increase them to lift them to the Christ. It is the beginning of spring. Feel yourself as the Cosmic Mother planting seeds of the spiritual realm in the ground.

EGO AND PERSONALITY RANGES

"Before the ego range, there was the learning of how to do things and how to handle the body. A person in the ego range suddenly knows many things and he goes out and tells what he knows. He seems to think he knows everything. When you see a person doing this, he is in the ego range. You just have to relax and let him go through this stage. Leave him alone and let him do what he wants to do.

"The ego range precedes the personality range. There are people who come in knowing. These are people who come in with awareness and they are usually very highly evolved. They are at least in the personality range, and they are perfecting the personality to use as a tool. Of course, you never really get completely through these stages since we carry with us remnants of different stages of development.

"So when you go into the personality range, you go into the creative stage where you learn how to handle the ego. Then you are ready to use what you've learned in the ego and personality ranges using the personality tool in the creative stage. Practically no one who has been given a brain radiation has been *completely* into this range except for daVinci, Ogamisama, and some of the saints. We always carry the personality.

ENERGY

"Energy that is brought up through the feet is magnetic earth energy which you can feel. It is the same as the energy one gets by grounding energy from a tree. It is good to go under trees and to walk barefoot on grass in order to release negative energy and to ground it. By taking limbs from two different branches and holding on to them, negative energy is automatically grounded. With this action, you get vital force that comes out of the tree and down through the hands and spine."

Dr. Pierce also taught that a person can ground his own energy by holding on to a hot and cold water faucet.

"Sending energy up through the feet can be done, being careful to use only the magnetic force of the earth. Ask for help from nature and the nature spirits. You can also lean against a tree by putting your spine against it to get energy. And sometimes, you get a tingly feeling in the palms or other areas of your body. You must always have your feet on grass or dirt so that the negative electricity will be grounded. Do this without shoes, although you may wear socks.

"A few people work with nature spirits. An example of this is found in Findhorn, Scotland. Every tree has a nature spirit or deva. I was amused one time when a friend said that she had been hit twice by the branches of a tree, by the deva of the tree, and she said that the deva did not like her. Every once in awhile you may feel antagonism from a plant. The devas are very protective. It is another dimension of our living.

"The feet and the hands play an important role as you bring in energy through them. Anything we do with our hands is creative. Spiritually, the feet represent wisdom. Biologically, they represent balance. When your feet are out of balance, then your wisdom is out of balance. So the feet are very important. Take good care of them and respect them as they are a balancing point of the body. Always move away from the person's feet when healing or cleansing the aura as you can pick up negativity from them. You may feel this negativity as a drop in vitality or being hit with something or feeling like you have the flu.

"It is very important to know that when you touch someone, an emanation goes out from your hands about two to three inches into the force field of the person. This is why it is important for you to watch what you do with your hands. Many people have an instinctive feeling about not touching people because of a concern about absorbing negativity.

FAILURE

"We must fail many times. A friend told me long ago that the only gift we really have is the chance to fail. I did not believe him, but I do now. Thank God for pain and failure. When we fail enough, we learn enough to know we do not know. It helps us take care of the ego and to be grateful for knowledge from anywhere.

GOD

"The Absolute called God is the great Principle. It is the sum of all intelligence, truth, love, and being. This means that all individual life, whether it be a person, a microbe, an electron, a star, or a planet—any life in the universe—all are bound and held together like drops of water in the ocean. The ocean has the power to sustain us, so does love. When we realize we are one with the Great Life, one with the Absolute and one with the great Principle, we are strong. And whenever we feel separate from life we feel alone, we lose our strength, and we are at the mercy of circumstances. This is not so because we have been told it. It is a law that we can never be alone.

GROUPS

"Once you start a group, you should not break the continuity of it. It is important to be present for the meeting. The group should continue even if only a few are present. Groups keep you mentally alert and growing. Every time someone new enters the group, he has to be absorbed into it, and become a part of it, before the flow of power becomes smooth and easy. We must have rapport, as everyone who works in the group is someone whose force field will intermingle. We are all in each other's force field. Every group develops a group entity unless broken.

"Whenever we, in any way, make any type of commitment or motion toward someone else, our vibration goes into them, into their force field, not into their auric field. You must have an affinity for the person you are working with. And remember, no one working with you can be negative. If I were angry with you, you would feel a portion of my anger.

"You can tell the members of a group almost anything, because if they aren't where they could hear it, they won't hear it. They will not know what you're saying; it has no meaning. This is why I feel you do not have to hide anything from people."

GROWTH

Spiritual development is singular. Each one of us develops individually in our own time. It is important to realize this in order to develop inner strength and power.

"The mood of 'The Dark Night of the Soul' is so difficult at the time, but good for us. Good growth factors require striving and the taking of responsibility for difficult things that come up, including stress and pain. Really, I don't know how one can grow without a lot of striving, a strong will, and determination to grow.

Then, spiritual consciousness becomes more than any other thing in importance. So, everything is within you. It really does not matter where you are because you go back to the understanding that ***we are all alone in time and space*** in our development anyway. Growth is a matter of desire. Emotion is the start. Motivation, intensity, and breathing are truly important for growth.

"It's only a facet that we are developing in this lifetime, and we have so much to learn. We do not know where we are, for the simple reason, that this is where we are in this lifetime. Next lifetime, it may be a completely different thing because we are developing this complete individual, and we will be in the situation that will give us the most development. This is why it is so important that we use everything we have to the best of our ability. We have so much to do in the time we have, and there is so much perfection that we have to have. We cannot compensate. We have to learn to do things perfectly. You do it. Perfect it. You drop it. You do not need it anymore.

HEALING

"All of us have the power to heal. All have the power to use this magnetic force that is both a physical magnetism and a healing power. Channel in power to yourself by using Light or Energy or Universal Consciousness; hold and use it. Feel it flow. Be kind, patient, and aware, which is not an easy task. Reach out an invisible finger and heal a person! It is best to use the power that comes into the hands but if you need to, you can use the physical magnetism. You can have a three-fold healing force, the Light, the power through the hand, and this magnetism which should not be done too often, as it takes energy from you. When a person gives a lot to people, love and approval may be needed in return. We are not aware of this enough. We need to be aware that people need this nurturing. Be sensitive enough to other's needs. Remember you must have an affinity for the person you are working on.

INDIVIDUAL

"No one is at home with all people. I meet people at their level when they come. If I cannot bring them into some kind of understanding of the Light, they soon go. Wherever you go, you build your own world. Know that you have the power to be whatever is necessary. Know that you are really one with God and this protects you. As spiritual knowledge flows from us, Light flows out. It's amazing when we really get the consciousness of some higher power being within us, how it helps, and there is no loneliness. I haven't been lonely in years. People and things become less important. As time goes on, only one's oneness with God becomes real.

"I am delighted that you are seeing and getting the proof of other dimensions of your being that is as real as today, and as real as the manifestation of your body. To know this and to know the love and protection of God means so much more than anything else does. Things may not happen which a person wants badly, so that there may be growth in another direction. We do not really have time to let the Spirit manifest. So many things; so much to do; we get so involved with them.

LIFE

"Life is truly short. Whatever happens will pass. It is hard to remember things that are for our growth and development, not that somewhere we failed.

"Not all people can see the same situation at the same time. There are some who cannot be on a spiritual path in this lifetime. Their evolution is not high enough. They must grow for a few lifetimes more.

"There is always in life a trial: during childhood, middle life, or old age. I think it is easier to handle when we are a little balanced and not so old.

"I am not so sure that helping others is not primarily helping oneself. Look for a way to use what you have and for new and creative ways to use it. We have so much we do not use or do. If only we could be more aware of what we do consciously or unconsciously. There are so many things that we don't know. Life is always up and down; however, if we look we find the magic. It is in the Light and leaves, in drops of rain, and in stones. Life is such a delightful, exciting, fantastic experience.

"It may be that I should retire from this life and take time to pray. Who knows? — I am really too busy now to think it out.

LOVE

"Love, which is produced as a work of thought, is usually less impersonal than creative energy. It is not the same as emotional energy. Every emotion has a reason. An example is love which is not creative energy in itself, but we can use love as a part of the creative energy in order to create with love when the love is impersonal and without attachment. You can also have an element of controlled anger in the creative force which gives it more impetus, more power, and sometimes more intensity, but first of all there has to be that creative urge. You can use the force of anger for good, which is positive, or for negative, but you have to have these forces under control. This is why you have impersonal love, which is love without attachment.

"You never let yourself get caught in any of these emotions. This is part of what we do when we control ego or control pride. This does not mean that you do not have pride in your work or anything you do. You want perfection and quality. You don't lose that part of it, but self-pride must be controlled. It then becomes humbleness and power, and the creative urge can come into the power of the individual spirit. This creative urge is sublimated and goes out as spiritual power that is used for the creation of the individual spirit. The spiritual essence that is created in the individual then is stored as spiritual essence and becomes a part of the soul.

MARRIAGE

"If ties (cords) are not cut, cleansed, and released between the child and each parent, the child is not free to have a good marriage.

ORGANS

"The pituitary gland, which has two functions, will do what it can do to balance, but it cannot do everything. When the pituitary gland is involved, it is very probable that other glands of the body will be affected, since there is an interrelationship between all glands. Until you are mature, the pituitary is the balancing gland of the body and it affects the growth of long bones. The anterior pituitary gland has to do with the heart, intestines, and uterus. It is a big factor for women in labor as it controls things. The posterior pituitary gland has to do with the metabolism of sugar and water. It controls the water balance of the body. The pancreas is involved with balance and helps to control sugar metabolism. The liver stores sugar and helps to balance sugar metabolism. Sugar affects the left lobe of the liver and inadvertently tears down the pancreas.

PATH

"It seems when we start on this path, there just is not any other. This I am sure.

POWER

"Your power lies within you and those with whom you work.

"There are differences in types of power, just as there are different types of energy. It is all power. Light is a type of power. Light is power. There is limitless power that we call Universal Consciousness. If we are receptive to it, we can bring it in through our left hand and feel it as heat. It comes up your arm and around the back of your head, over your shoulders, and out your right hand, and you can use it for healing, for purifying, and for cleansing negativity. It is directed with the right hand and it is received with the left hand. There is a star position that brings the power in faster. You stand with your feet apart, and you put your hands out and postulate that there is a power and that you feel it now. A second position is to sit and hold your hands, palms up, on your knees.

"The power comes in through my left and sometimes it cramps the muscles on my left arm, and sometimes it is like a hot ball in the center of the palm. If you send the Light into the person, ask that it be tempered to meet his needs so that you do not send too much power. If you send love, it is automatically tempered. This is a healing power that we have and that we use for healing. I use this when I treat people. Postulate that the person's tissues are intelligent and aware and will be attentive and receptive. Tissues that become aware heal faster. My left hand is uplifted and my right palm is on the abdomen. The power usually goes across the shoulders, and it usually comes in from the left. Many times if you are left-handed, it comes in from the right. This power is the Universal Power. It is the same power that we call **fohat**, which is vital force or energy. It has small microscopic diamond-shaped areas which flash in White Light. When you are very high spiritually and very aware, you see this. This is the power, the vital living force in man. We bring this power in when we breathe. This power gives us life force and energy. When it touches the body, it comes in as the vital breath through the nose, throat, skin, pores, and the top of the head.

"Power works at two levels of consciousness, the physical and the etheric. The vital force comes in through the pineal, is stepped down by the thymus and is sent out through the body by the spleen. In Chinese medicine, the spleen is the organ of the distribution of this life force. It is very important to work with the thymus. If there is impairment in the thymus, the patient is tired and depleted, and the vital force is impaired. If the thymus is too impaired, the patient dies. And if the patient dies, it is not because of the thymus, but because of the fact that he could not get this vital energy which comes down through the top of the head to the spleen, and it could not get distributed throughout the body. The person is still getting energy through the skin, but it is not enough.

"The vital force must come in and go through the central nervous system and through the glands. The glandular system is very important. The liver is the gland of the emotions. The thymus is the gland that is called vital life. This gland is an important aspect of the bringing in of our vital energy.

POWER OF THE WORD

"The Light has to be visualized as you say it. The spoken word has so much power and also the power of the word itself, and this is why it's so important that we are careful what we say about people and to people. We visualize the Light with the power of the word and it makes it very strong. Visualization is thinking, and if you can see it, it is a manifestation of the word. If you can visualize it while you are saying it, it becomes more quickly a fact.

REALITY

"Leave people to their own reality.

"Be careful of taking on the energy of the person who is despondent.

"What you put out comes back to you.

RELATIONSHIP

"It is hard to face things, but if they threaten a friendship, it is best to talk it out and see what you can do. One has to play it by ear and treat the present time problems first. We have to judge what we feel is important to us, a surface relationship or an in-depth one. It is not easy. We must have patience and compassion.

RESPONSIBILITY

"Responsibility and decision are interlaced. It is better to make a poor decision than to make no decision. The decision must be made. It is a part of the growth. I was told once that the only thing we are born with is the ability to make mistakes, because we learn by the gift of making mistakes. If you do not make any mistakes, you never learn. Occasionally, there will be a person who just does not make any mistakes. For this lifetime, he has either good or bad karma. He develops no merit. In the problem lies the answer; in the problem lies the growth. It is the problem that makes us grow, that pushes us into something else. It forces you into many things you would not do without it. Responsibility is the acceptance of a moral or physical obligation.

SPIRITUAL ESSENCE

"This is not *prana* or *fohat*. *Fohat* and *prana* are things that come as a vital force for living. They are the living life forces that come into the individual. We can take in more or less life force as we breathe. This life force that I am talking about is the essence, the growth of the Spirit that makes a larger spiritual consciousness that you will take with you when you go over into transition, and that you carry with you from incarnation to incarnation. You have the choice to grow or not to grow. The individual who is asleep sometimes makes no spiritual essence during this lifetime. In this spiritual essence lies the growth of the individual, and this is the **soul growth** that we accomplish so very slowly.

"With this spiritual essence comes the growth of the Spirit and this is the Godlike quality; this is the spiritual quality of the human being. If you have enough of this spiritual quality, you will go over as a big person. Many times, the very humble person in this lifetime who doesn't seem to be anything at all, in the next lifetime will be a powerful spiritual leader, a spiritual giant. The person has gotten so much spiritual essence that he or she has been developing Spirit throughout his or her lifetime.

"This is an important factor because it is this essence that we carry on as soul and Spirit growth. This is the purpose of this lifetime that we don't know much about, and we don't realize the importance of soul growth. Our values have not been right; they have been misplaced. What we need is growth of the soul and Spirit. We get some of this essence inadvertently. The right sexual relationship is a beautiful thing that happens between two people. There is some spiritual essence there. When you go through pain or sorrow or turmoil, if you choose the situation in the right way, you get spiritual essence. If you use your concentration completely, you grow spiritual essence.

TEACHER

"We seldom meet more than one strong teacher in our lifetime.

"Each teacher gives something. Remember, a teacher is for now. Then take from the next one, as there may be for you the rare magic of finding a wise and holy man who is in a space where he can change your consciousness. For this we pray. Remember, prayer is the soul's sincere desire. Look for people who speak to your soul. Once in a lifetime, we may find one who plays the divine melody of infinite knowledge. For now the desire to know guides us.

"Listen to your center. Any man is your teacher; let him teach.

"Send out your **Golden Ray of Wisdom and Knowledge** from your mind to heal. Touch men's souls. Remember you are a part of God.

TRUTH

If there is a question, look at it very carefully. Take thought. There is always our truth for now. It may not be for someone else.

Take your own truth, only that which you understand. Do not feel duty-bound to take someone else's reality until you understand it. The path is so exciting. There is so much to learn.

"The more aware you become, the more you can realize, and the more you get. Suddenly, a flow of direct knowledge comes to you.

"To know truth is the beginning of all knowledge. We have to remember *we are all alone in time and space.*"

Chapter II

THE USE OF LIGHT AND POWER

> "May the peace and joy of the Spirit be with you
> now and always."
> —Gayle C. Pierce

Dr. Pierce was frequently asked to do prayer and healing for others. The following sections include information on healing, and the specific prayers which individuals received as a result of these requests. It is essential that the rudiments of her work are understood before helping the person in need.

A healing must always be in agreement with the desire and consent of the person receiving the healing. When using White Light, always temper the Light according to the person's needs. In all healings, *visualization* is necessary.

INDIVIDUAL HEALINGS

"Ask that the Power come into the room to bring power and protection to the person receiving the healing.

"Bring in the Light according to what the individual understands. For many people, the Christ Light is what is understood. **This Light is a brilliant, living, golden color.**

"For an Indian person, bring in Light. For the Muslim, bring in the Light of Prophet Mohammed, which is **Golden Light.** The White Light of the Living God may be used for anyone regardless of belief. It is good to visualize for the person, both the color and the state of consciousness needed for the healing.

"Ask that the Universal Presence enter the room and that it purify and cleanse the individual's body, soul and Spirit. If anything else needs to be cleansed, it can be stated at that time.

1. Fear of Life

"We ask that (person's name) come in, and we ask that he stand for inspection. We hold him in the Light, the Light of Awareness and the Light of Understanding.

"We ask (repeat name) that you take a step forward, knowing that you are here in this lifetime. Be aware that you must do the best you can with what you have, for now. We ask that the Light of the Spirit be in and around you, making you conscious that you have the ability to step forward and giving you a knowingness that this is what must be done. We ask that the fear of anything that might be there be taken away. The White Light goes through you. The wall of Living Flame is built completely around and about you so that it passes under your feet and encompasses you and your aura in a protective Light, giving you courage, understanding, and awareness.

"As the Light goes on the feet, this individual grows from a three-year-old to a fourteen-year-old in consciousness. This person's fear had inhibited his emotional and mental maturation. (In this case it was necessary to reinforce the Light by putting it around him again).

"The Light goes through him, around him, about him, through his feet and under his feet. And let it be where he walks so that he may walk with sureness and with knowledge, and that whatever is done is the most he can receive for now. We send this Light around him again, reinforcing and giving him love, understanding, and companionship.

"We send Light, love, and understanding to the feet. (Name), be aware, be good to yourself and take care of your feet. Know that as you take each step there is a God consciousness and your knowledge of the beingness of the man you are goes with you, and as you go toward the Light, and always go toward the Light, know it will be there. And we bid you good night, and we release you.

2. Light and Health

"We ask that the Light go through (person's name) and neutralize anything that is not for (repeat name) highest good. We ask for health and understanding and that the gold Light bring (repeat name) health and knowledge.

3. Working with the Light in Distant Areas

"We place the Golden Bridge of Understanding in New Delhi, and we send Light from here to New Delhi. We can ask that a being help us in that area, and we can ask the Guardian Angel of the area involved to keep guard over anything that is touched in our work."

EMERGENCY POWER AND PROTECTION

"For emergency power and protection, bring in the Flame of the Spirit which is to be used only on yourself. Place it around the body. For others, use the White Light. If people's anger or negative thought patterns are aimed at and get attached to us, check behind the liver which is the emotional center. Cut away all cords using the Light and Sword of the Spirit."

The Flame of the Spirit is an apricot-colored ray of Light.

OBSTRUCTIONS

An obstruction may be a shadow, a negative force, or an emotional blockage around a person or situation. If the person doing healing work is unable to remove the obstruction, then the following statement must be said: "If I am not to do this work, I ask that the obstruction leave immediately, and I place the power and the Light of protection around me."

"Make a mesh bag of gold or White Light and put into it the substance to be gotten rid of, and send it out into space. Or, you can make a bag of gold, silver, or iron and put the White Light around the obstruction. That makes it more stationary. Ask that it no longer bother anyone, and ask that it be wrapped in White Light and sent out into space. Then if it is supposed to stay, it will, and if it isn't to stay, it will be dissolved."

No work regarding obstruction is to be done without the following statement: "If this is not my work, then I ask that it leave."

"Always ask where the obstruction is located. Then the White Light must be put through the situation or the object or the image. If the Light does not go through the obstruction, put the Cross of the Living Christ through it. (This is the Equidistant Cross)."

UNWELCOME INTRUSION

When someone else's negative thoughts are being directed at you, place a transparent glass wall between the two of you. If this is not sufficient, place a transparent glass bell over the person. If this is still not sufficient, place a glass bell over yourself as well as the other person. The glass wall and bell previously lasted as a protection for approximately twenty-four hours. Now it is a much shorter time because the Light on the planet has intensified. Both the bell and the wall dissipate when no longer needed. The use of the glass wall or bell may be repeated as necessary. This procedure is particularly helpful when someone's energies are adversely affected.

The following steps are to be used when dealing with an unwelcome intrusion:

1. Command by statement that whoever is there has no business being there and that it return from whence it came.

2. Place an Equidistant Cross between yourself and the unwelcome intrusion.

3. Intensely visualize the Golden Light of Christ (buttercup yellow) or the Light of any divine being with whom you have a relationship.

4. Pour the very bright Gold Light of knowledge and healing through the situation.

5. Demand that the intrusion leave.

6. "If the intrusion refuses to leave, say: 'In the name of the Christ Consciousness, I demand that you leave.' If the intrusion still refuses to leave, then this command must be stated a third time. The Sign of the Cross may be used when making the demand, or the demand may be made in the name of Jesus the Christ. The demand may also be made in the name of God. If the intrusion is in someone's aura, use the truly brilliant White Light.

"The following statement must be spoken when working with an intrusion that refuses to leave: 'If it is mine, I transmute it. If it is not mine, I demand that it be released and returned from whence it came.'"

If an intrusion refuses to leave, asking is not enough. A demand must be made.

The symptoms of psychic attack include confused thinking, loss of striving, loss of will, unexplained fatigue, and the perception of jagged lines of light.

A NEGATIVE IMPINGEMENT

"A feeling of not being able to think can be a negative thing that has been thrown at us. It can be a thought form and it impinges on the Desire Body or the aura, and it can affect a person physically. The thing to do is to stop right then and put on the Armor of Light; use the Golden Light and put Ogamisama's Golden Light behind and in front of you. Or, you can use the power of the Christ Consciousness or the Power of the Cross or Buddhic Consciousness or Ogamisama's Consciousness. Ask that the negative impingement be dispelled. It is also good to use a symbol such as the Golden Disc (a shield) and demand in the name of God that this impingement go from (name)."

The Desire Body consists of a person's feelings, desires, wishes, and emotions.

"You have the power to clean up your aura and your own desire body, as you have the power to clean up anything else. Ask that your auric field be cleansed, that your desire body be cleansed, and that anything that is not yours, leave you. Become aware that these things do happen and take care of them immediately. Someone can throw a very nasty dagger of a thought at you, and it impinges on the auric field, so the first thing you should do is to cleanse your aura with Light and demand that anything not for your good be released from your aura. No one has the right to throw this kind of negative thought at you, and we have the right to use this power and make a demand that anything be released from our aura. We have the power to do this and **within us is the Power.** Demand the release in the name of the God consciousness."

Chapter III

METHODS OF PROTECTION

> "Within you is the Light."
>
> —Gayle C. Pierce

BRINGING IN THE POWER

"Cleanse and strengthen your aura each day by putting on the **Armor of Light.** Place an armor of Gold Light around the bottom of your feet, bringing it up and around your head and shoulders. You should do this especially when working with people. Ask that your bodies be aligned. Then bring the Light down through your heart center, which clears your force field."

There are several energetic bodies. They include the physical, astral, etheric, and mental.

"Bring in the Christ Consciousness which is the color of buttercup gold. After tempering the White Light say, 'Let the rose-red

Light be filled in the entire whole of the auric field and let it spread out as protection.' This may be used for the entire body including the seven chakras, and particularly for the heart and sex centers by taking the rose-red Light and affirming that it goes throughout the body. Cobalt blue may also be used to help awareness and spiritual consciousness.

"White Light, when used for cleansing, **must be tempered for adults, children, and animals.** There is no reason to temper the Light when cleansing the environment or objects.

"When working with both awareness and spiritual consciousness, visualize a very small deep blue flame in the heart. See it grow, expand, and come up through the throat, mouth, ears, and eyes—no farther. As the flame expands it will become lighter."

Using a crystal ball as a focus helps to maintain clarity of concentration.

"Build a fire at least once a month. Use the fire to affirm the Golden Path and to take out negative vibrations.

A.M. Put your feet together. Then sit in a figure eight (cross-legged) position up to the knees. Feel that your feet are planted in the earth. This is a method of establishing a connection with the earth in order to maintain mental clarity and a clear focus. Postulate that you are grounding yourself by saying 'I am grounding myself.' Grounding is a form of protection. It encourages focus and concentration. After grounding, uncross your legs.

P.M. Prior to sleep, ask to be protected in White and Golden Light. Ask for the protection angel as you go to sleep at night. You can take its hand.

"Each morning before you get up, bring the world of Light into your body. You bring the Light into your body by filling your body with Light, and visualizing your body as being completely vibrant and alive with Light that is lighter than clouds, scintillating, bright and sparkling. It is a clear, vibrant light, not thick like a cloud. It comes in almost like a light ray. Also, bring the golden-apricot Light of the Flame of the Spirit up, over, and through the feet, body, crown, and over and through the auric field."

When using the Flame of the Spirit, it is usually brought from the feet upward, as if stepping into a flame.

NEGATIVITY

"We must be aware of the negativity that comes in through the feet, and we must use our feet as centers of Light, so that the Light streams out and dispels and disperses darkness as we walk.

"The more negativity an individual has, the more negativity he can project in his attack. The thought form hovers over you and shuts off part of your ability because it impinges on the Desire

Body. The Desire Body, because it is Light and because of its beauty, will attract these things. You have to put up a shield; you have to be aware; you have to protect yourself. The more Light you have the more negativity is attracted to it. If desired, a mantra such as Aum, Om or the Tibetan Hum may be chanted. Aum, Om, and Hum symbolize God, the creator and sustainer of all things, the prime vibration."

PRAYERS OF PROTECTION

Over the years the following prayers, particularly the "Armor Of Light," were spoken aloud at the group meetings in Dr. Pierce's home.

God, Jesus Christ, or another spiritual being may be thought of in the following prayers:

ARMOR OF LIGHT: ARMOR OF GOD

The "Armor of Light" appears as a dazzling White Light. The "Armor of Light" has variations. It may be used for the protection of all modes of transportation. A strong visualization of putting on this "Armor of Light" intensifies the prayer.

"In the name and through the power and by the word of the Living Christ, I put on the whole Armor of Light. On my head is the helmet of salvation. I wear the breastplate of righteousness. My loins are girded with the Truth. My feet are shod in peace and enveloped in the Flame of the Spirit of Almighty God. In my left hand I hold the shield of faith. In my right hand is the Sword of the Spirit which is the Word of God. The Word of God is unassailable and no evil shall come nigh my habitation *(or my vehicle of transportation)*. Thus clad I stand, joyfully expectant, ready to do the will of the Father."

Adapted from Ephesians 6:10-18

WALL OF LIVING FLAME

"In the name and through the power and by the Word of the Living Christ, I put a Wall of Living Flame around me *(other people, vehicles, and material objects may be included)*, and I give thanks that it is done. Amen.

"In the name and through the Power and by the Word of Jesus Christ, a Wall of Living Flame is built around me, and I give thanks to the Father."

The "Wall of Living Flame" prayers of protection are particularly appropriate when immediate protection is necessary. Enclose others in the vehicle, as well as the luggage, in the Wall of Living Flame.

WALK IN THE LIGHT

"May we walk in the Light,
May we become one with the Light,
And may the Peace and the Joy of the Spirit
Be with us now and always."

[Dr. Pierce closed each meditation group with this prayer.]

CLOTHED IN LIGHT

"I walk in Light, armored and clothed in Light.
I breathe it in with every breath I draw,
And thus I become more like the Father
Who is Light Eternal."

CLEANSING OF BUILDINGS AND OBJECTS

Fifty feet was appropriate for both cleansing buildings and personal protection in the 1970s. Now, it is mandatory to take the Light farther above the buildings and more deeply into the ground, i.e. *at least 1000 feet <u>or more</u>.* The Light has a very high vibratory frequency and in this time of the New Age the Light is much more quickly dissipated; therefore, a farther reaching Light is necessary in order to dispel anything that is not of the Light. **This information applies to all statements in the book where a number less than 1000 feet is used for protection.**

Dr. Pierce used the following prayers for the cleansing of buildings, houses, offices, land, objects, negativity, and for anything or anyone having a negative vibration.

I

"We ask that the White Light of the Universal Consciousness go into this building, and that the Angel of Light with the Flaming Sword of the Spirit karmically go into this office, cleansing, revitalizing, and completely cleaning out negativity. Let it go in every corner, in every cupboard, in every space, and let a Wall of Living Flame be put in this office to protect it from negativity, and let it go through the vibrations of every person who comes into this office to help neutralize the negativity of each individual. Let it go down into the floor, leaving in each space a Living Flame, a Golden Flame of the Spirit that cleanses, purifies, and revitalizes the whole of the atmosphere. Let there be a wall of protection going around the office. Let it be cleansed, purified and completely neutralized of anything that is negative. Let each person be aware of his own negativity and let the negativity that is left in this office be dissolved, cleansed, and neutralized. We ask that this be done in the name of the Power of the Golden Flame of Ogamisama and the Golden Ray of Ogamisama, and we leave the form of **Na-myo-ho-ren-ge-kyo** written in the air over every door and written on every window, and let it remain a part of the atmosphere of this building, cleansing, purifying and neutralizing.

"We cleanse each of us, and we establish our wall of protection so that none of the negativity that was in this building will come at us. Let the Flame of the Spirit go around our feet and wherever we walk. May we cleanse and purify with the Flame of the Spirit that flows through and out of the feet 50 feet into every step we take, and 50 feet beneath us, and may it flow through these 50 feet cleansing and purifying, and may it protect us from any negativity coming in through the feet."

> *Na-myo-ho-ren-ge-kyo is a chant received by Ogamisama from the One (God) after He entered into her body. Loosely translated, it means "A little known person received this from the Almighty". She was told to repeat this chant one hundred times daily. Na-myo-ho-ren-ge-kyo has the power to redeem negativity. It is a prayer for the sake of all mankind. Ogamisama said that when all negativity is redeemed, world peace will occur.*

II

"Let the house of (name) be cleansed and completely neutralized of negativity. We ask that her children and her family, and Mr. (name) be given Universal Light and the White Light of Universal Consciousness, that the thirteen-year-old daughter be stabilized by the Universal Light and the White Light of Universal Consciousness. We ask that the White Light go 50 feet above the house and 50 feet under the house, and surround the house, that the whole of this situation is cleansed in the Light."

Ask that the Light go through the house cleansing and purifying. Name the rooms including the basement. Cleanse the walls and the furniture and ask that the Light permeate 50 feet or more into the ground.

III

"We ask that the Flaming Sword of the Spirit go through this house, cleansing and transmuting it into Light.

IV

"We ask that the Flaming Sword of the Spirit go through this house cleansing and transmuting into Light anything that is not of the Light. We ask that this Light go 50 feet into the ground, cleansing, purifying and permeating all walls, objects and debris."

Do the cleansing from room to room, naming each room. The preferable method of cleansing is from the roof of the house, then through the house, the basement and into the ground.

V

In the following sections, the dialogue between Dr. Pierce and the author is identified as Dr. P and C, respectively. During these sessions, some of the responses by the author were not captured on tape.

Dr. P: We send the Light that is a part of all things to C's home. We send the Light of Universal Consciousness which will grow and be a center of Light and Understanding so that whatever she starts in this new apartment she can finish, and it may become a thing of power for her, so we ground this apartment for her and give her a center of peace, a center of understanding, and a center of love.

VI

Looking at someone's house where a part of the house is clear and a part of it is cloudy.

Dr. P: Let's send White Light where the cloudiness is, and the Flaming Sword into this house, cleansing and purifying, neutralizing all negativity and all darkness, bringing only Light and understanding.

Dr. P (to C): See what you see there.

Dr. P: We will cleanse the house and this family and put a wall of protection around them and send them peace, knowing that whatever is best for this household and this family will happen. And we will now send the Light and the Seal of the Christ Consciousness into this family and into this home.

Dr. P (to C): Is this a psychic pain, or is this an entity, or is this a condition? Is it in the body itself?

C: (describes to Dr. P what she sees in the organs.)

Methods of Protection

Dr. P: I ask that anything that possesses (name's) bowel or anything in any way impairing her health or anything concerning her be brought to our attention. We ask you to leave in the name of the Christ Consciousness. We ask you to leave and let this woman be free. Again we send the Light of the Christ Consciousness to (name), giving her peace and complete health, and we ask that you who are over her leave and set her free, and that you go back from whence you came, leaving (name) free to do the thing that is necessary for her to do.

Dr. P (to C): What kind of person do you see?

C: (describes what she sees)

Dr. P: We ask that whoever this is, to leave her body, to set her free, and we ask that the White Light cleanse her body, leaving her to do whatever is necessary. And to this person (the attacker), let the Light go through him, guiding him to do what he needs to do.

(Cleansing begins to take place.)

Dr. P: We ask that the White Light go through him and that a wall of Living Flame be placed between them. We ask that the Light cleanse, and purify, and release him to go back to wherever he needs to go. We thank the healers and helpers for taking him away; thank you for the cleansing. We go and leave her in peace. We ask that this protection be placed around her; that she be released to do whatever good she has to do; that she do it with love and with understanding. We ask that the Light of the Christ

Consciousness and the Sign of the Cross be placed on the whole of her body tonight, particularly the liver, spleen, heart, and the back of the head. We release her with peace, and thank you very much for the help.

VII

Dr. P: We ask that if (name) can step into the Light, we can then see what is bothering her. We ask at this time that the protection, the wall of Living Flame, be reinforced around the house and be reinforced around us, and that nothing can enter, and that we are completely encompassed with this Flame of the Spirit, and that it is a protection against any negativity.

VIII

Dr. P (to C): Ask the family member to come in as she sincerely wishes to resolve the problem between them for the goodness of both parties.

C: I ask her to step into the Light now and to return weekly along with the other family member in order to filter out some of the feelings that they have not talked about.

Chapter IV

RELEASING AND CUTTING CORDS

> "We operate at many levels of consciousness."
>
> —Gayle C. Pierce

When cutting cords, a pair of golden shears or scissors or the Sword of the Spirit may be used.

Begin with the statement: "I take the Sword of the Spirit (or shears or scissors) and I cut and neutralize the cords between the person or the persons involved, and the situation."

Many cases involved the release of individuals from situations that occurred on the physical plane. Other cases involved the release of persons who had passed on but who were still bound by earthly ties. The knowledge of knowing how to effectively release and cleanse both the situation and the people involved is of utmost importance in order to complete the release of all involved.

The work of cutting cords is also of great importance because the person remains bound to the earth until the cords are cut, neutralized, released and transmuted; however, sometimes cords cannot be neutralized, purified and released from the person who originated the situation because this is tampering with the person's karma.

TAMPERING WITH A SITUATION THAT SHOULD HAVE BEEN LEFT ALONE

Dr. P: We ask that (person's name) be put in Light. We ask that the Master Kuthumi and the Master Moraya take over the cleansing of (name), and that they take care of her and do whatever is necessary to bring the Light of the Spirit. We ask that this be done tonight. We place her in the Light of the Spirit with the Golden Ray of Healing and of Knowledge coming to her, so she will know right from wrong, and she will know when she is tampering with something she should leave alone. And we ask that her Guardian Angel protect her and give her more awareness. We ask at this time that the protection of a wall of Living Flame go around (name) and her home, and that it go through her and cleanse her and purify her and that an extra wall of Living Flame come around this house, protecting us and protecting the house so that no negativity can enter here. And we thank you.

A SITUATION INVOLVING A WOMAN WHO HAS PASSED ON BUT HER HUSBAND AND SON ARE LIVING

Dr. P: We ask at this time, if (person's name) is willing, that she come into the room, and we will see if we can help her.

C: I see her leg dragging.

Dr. P (to C): The person died of a heart attack.

C: I see inconsistencies in the right and left sides.

Dr. P (to C): She has not the awareness yet and is still relating to the body.

Dr. P: (apologizes for not getting to this sooner)

Dr. P: We ask that all ties with the earth be cut, and that you be released from the earth, and we ask again that the Archangel Raphael come in and heal you, that he take you within his wings, and take the spiritual consciousness of (person's name) to a higher consciousness, a larger awareness, and to more knowledge, and we let her go toward the Light, releasing all things here.

Dr. P: (feels that the person has bitterness)

Dr. P: All the ties that hold you, we cut them using a pair of golden scissors. We cut all the ties of all the people that hold you to earth, including your mother and your sister. And now the Archangel Raphael will heal you and take you to the Light. You understand and know, and you go toward the Light and creativity, and you will arise glorious and shining. Let them minister to you and let the Light shine about you and over you, and let the Spirit that is you become a thing of beauty and of peace, and let all the colors of the rainbow heal you and nourish you and give you joy. So we release you tonight in the name of the Christ Consciousness and in the name of Archangel Raphael for healing and for growth.

Dr. P: We ask that the Light of the Spirit be around (person's name) son and (person's name) husband be cleansed of all things where his wife is concerned, that anything that is his go back to him, that anything that is hers go back to her, and that it go back cleansed and purified so that he has no memories except happy ones, and no grief, and we ask particularly that the son leave the memory of his mother in peace, and that he think of her only in beauty, and that his Spirit has only joy and understanding. And we ask that this be done in the name of the Light. We cut the cords of all of the men in her life, cleansing them, and releasing them, leaving only happiness and joy. And we ask that the Light go through her situation, wherever it may be. (***Na-myo-ho-ren-ge-kyo*** is chanted several times).

A SITUATION WHERE A LIVING PERSON POSSESSES BOTH STRONG FORCES OF LIGHT AND STRONG FORCES OF DARKNESS

Dr. P: I ask that the White Light of the Universal Consciousness go through these forces of darkness, neutralizing and transmuting them. I ask that they be completely gone. In the name of the Christ Consciousness, I command you to be gone, and in the name of the Cross I command you to completely leave this girl. And I ask that the White Light of the Spirit flow through her and around her, completely encompassing her, going from the top of the head down the spine, cleansing her with the White Light and taking all of the symptoms from her.

MALE ON THE OTHER SIDE (Deceased)

Dr. P: We ask that any cords that are attached to (name) on this earth plane be cut and severed with the Sword of the Spirit, and those cords that are hers go back to her and that the cords be transmuted in Light, and those cords that are not hers be returned to (name) who is on the other side.

We ask that the cords be cut and returned to whomever they belong, and that they be completely released from both of them and that they both be completely free. He is on the other side, and this matter will be taken care of along with everything else. The other cords must go back to wherever they go, and may they be cleansed, and may his wife be given comfort and understanding as the cords she sent are returned to her so that she can have a fuller and more complete life.

MOTHER ON THE OTHER SIDE

Dr. P: Now we ask that the mother of (person's name) come into the Light if she is willing and come in to have all earth ties cut. We send for her with love. (The mother wants to know what we want). We ask you if there is anything you want to release, and we will release it.

We ask that all earth ties be released from you so that you can go on to any evolution or any growth factor. We ask that the Light of the protecting angels guide you and that you go on to your growth in your world of Light and understanding. We ask that the cords from your mother, your father, your former husband, and your child be released, and whatever is there that is theirs go back to them and that you be permitted to go on your way in understanding and with love.

We ask that your mother be cleansed and purified and be released to go on her way so that she can do whatever is necessary, and that the Light of Universal Consciousness go through her, giving her the power to do her own growth, and giving her the power to go wherever it is necessary. And we ask that the White Light and the Gold Light of the Christ Consciousness go through her and about her, cutting any cords with anyone, giving her peace and the Growth of the Spirit, and that nothing has a right to stop her.

(Person's name), you have the right to go forward, and no one has the right to stop you. So, step forward into peace and Light, and we ask that the Archangel Raphael help you with any ties that may need to be broken or any reinforcement of courage or any healing that is necessary. Then we release you for tonight.

C: There is some more trouble here. (C asks about a relative).

Dr. P: For tonight, (person's name), mother of (child's name), we release you to the Light. Thank you for coming.

A LIVING DAUGHTER: HER MOTHER ON THE OTHER SIDE

Dr. P: We ask that the desire body of (person's name) come in and that she come in with the Golden Light of Ogamisama so that we may help her in any way that we can with any of her problems. We ask that the ties between the daughter and her mother that are not for their best interests be cut, and the things of the mother go back to her, and the things that are the daughter's return to her, and that all things be cleansed between them.

Look clearly but honestly at any emotions about your mother. We ask that the Light go through you, cleansing scars, memories, and anything that is necessary at this time. We ask that you keep your own reality and release your mother to hers.

Ogamisama says that after telling someone a truth three times, we must release that person to his own reality, that it is our responsibility, even to our family, to release the person, and to let him go to the thing that he must do and the thing that must happen to him, and that we can't take him beyond a certain point. We do what we have to do, but only to that point do we do it, so we ask that the mother be released to her responsibility, and the daughter be released to hers so that she can keep her own reality and not get caught up in her mother's. If it is the mother's karmic debt, it is the mother's karmic debt. We only do what the person's soul will let us do. We cannot go beyond it. We only ask that they stand in the Light to receive help if possible.

And so we release you, (mother's name), to go with love and understanding in whatever way you can go, but we release the Light to work with more understanding if you wish to take it, and with more power if you wish it.

INQUIRY REGARDING A LIVING FEMALE

Dr. P: We ask that (person's name) step into the Light if she is willing, and that the guardian angel bring her and protect her.

Dr. P (to C): Please look and see what (person's name) is doing, and if we are to do anything about this.

C: We are to leave this alone.

Dr. P: We ask that the Flame of the Spirit go through (person's name). We ask that you leave with love, understanding and Power. We put the White Light and the Light of the Universal Power and Consciousness around you. Good night, (person's name). Go in love.

LIVING WIFE: HUSBAND ON THE OTHER SIDE

Dr. P: And now, we look at whatever is necessary for (person's name) health and the ties between her and her husband. We ask that she release him so that he becomes self-sufficient, and we ask that anything that is earthbound be released and that Mrs. (name) have peace of mind and a sense of well-being so that she feels she is healthy and well and capable. And let her find a sense of fun. Let the power of the White Light of the Universal Consciousness and the Golden Light of Ogamisama be around her so that she is aware of its warmth and its healing. And in this let her find her own life force, and let her become a part of it. At the same time let the light of Ogamisama go through her, cleansing her and cleansing anything in her desire body, anything that shouldn't be there and anything that is there that is not completely clear. Let her see and clearly understand this release.

LIVING SON AND HUSBAND: WIFE ON THE OTHER SIDE

Dr. P: We wish to have the healers and helpers bring (person's name) into the Light so that we know how (person's name) is progressing on the other side. We ask you to keep your hands off your son for you must realize that it is not your place to hold him down; he is not in the same place as you, and he has a job to do.

C: The woman seems to be in the dark and does not know what to do, and her helpers aren't helping her much.

Dr. P: We ask that the angels of Light come to her, and we ask that the memories of pain from the stroke be cleansed so that she can begin to grow on the other side. We also ask that the cords extending to her son and husband be cut and severed.

We ask for the guardian angels to minister to the husband and son and to help them be aware of their angels.

Releasing and Cutting Cords

Building dedicated to Dr. Pierce
(resident nunnery)
Gelukpa Tradition
Dharamsala, India

Chapter V

PRAYER AND MEDITATION

"All paths lead to God."

—Gayle C. Pierce

PRAYER

"When praying:

1. Sit where the vibrations are best for you.

2. Bring in the Triune Ray (Love, Light and Life) which neutralizes actions of negativity.

3. Cleanse and protect the room, then cleanse yourself.

4. Sit still. When praying, before doing spiritual work, ask for whoever needs work done to come into the Light. Then, let the questions regarding the person come through your intuition.

5. Firmly get the question in mind; then ask yourself the question as if you were the second person. Postulate that you will know what questions to ask.

6. Be sure to dismiss the people you have worked with after the prayer work has been completed. Thank them and affirm that the Light comes through them in their situation."

The Triune Ray is known as the "Power of Powers". It is a combination of three rays: God the Father who is Love, the Son who is Life, and the Holy Spirit who is Light. This Ray can be used to cleanse, to bless, and to heal. Because it is so powerful a vibration, it <u>must</u> be tempered according to the spiritual unfoldment of those to whom it is sent. This includes the person who is bringing it in as he must attune himself to the Triune Ray when he uses it. Tempering is most effective when it is vocalized. The Triune Ray is composed of three colors, each with its own rate of vibration. These colors are:

1. Sapphire-blue for healing—signified by the Ray of Love, represented by the Angel Gabriel.

2. White for cleansing, purifying, and revealing the obscure, represented by the Archangel Michael.

3. Gold for the Ray of Life—represented by the Angel Azrael, who separates the soul from the body at the time of the person's departure from the earth plane. Azrael has been

called the Angel of Death in both the Hebrew and Islamic traditions.

It was customary to light candles and burn incense before the group meditation began. Dr. Pierce recited the following prayer or a version of it, as it varied from meditation to meditation. "We come together in a community of Light. We come together in a community of striving. We come together in a community of love. We ask for awareness and we ask for God consciousness."

With dedication, she requested the presence of the Light to come into the room to give whatever was needed. This was followed by the recitation of the prayer of protection, "Armor of Light". The angelic realm, and the healers and helpers were then called upon. Sometimes the angels of the North, East, South, and West were brought in to protect the four directions, the room, and the people in it. The angels of Light usually came from the East. They were asked to remain for the duration of the meeting. Their presence lifted the energy of the room and enabled those in the group to receive teachings at a deeper level of understanding then they would normally experience. Even with the angels' presence, the capacity of understanding varied with each individual. Occasionally, specific angels entered the room because of a particular need of the group. Dr. Pierce stated that an angel could spread its feathered wings around the person needing help. She described these feathers as "a shimmer of light".

Prayer work was occasionally done for those needing spiritual assistance. Dr. Pierce often taught that if a person was not yet ready to receive that help, seeds of understanding were sent to the individual's auric field so that when the person was capable, at whatever evolutionary stage, the help would become apparent. In praying for someone, when something could not be done at that time to help either the person or the circumstances, then the Light could be sent to be used by the person at a future time if he accepted it. This was of utmost importance because we could not ask that a person be healed or that an obstacle be removed unless we affirmed that whatever was done, was done in accordance with the person's highest desire and for the good of all concerned. We were not to interfere with the lesson that the individual needed to learn, as not only was it against the spiritual law but we could absorb some of the person's karma as well.

Of significant importance was a protection prayer (Chapter III) to be placed around and about the person doing the work as well as around the person who was receiving spiritual assistance. This was necessary because the person doing the healing could also absorb the emotional content of the person being healed, including the person's attitudes, perceptions, and negativity.

Another example of a prayer invocation which Dr. Pierce recited at the beginning of a meditation is:

"We come together in a Community of Prayer. We come together in a Community of Light. We come together in a Community of Friendship. We come together in a Community of Love. We ask for awareness, we ask for God Consciousness. We ask at this time that the Light come into this room, into the center of the circle—the Light of the Flame of the Spirit. And we ask that this Flame remain in the center of the room for protection and for healing, for the work that we are to do tonight. May this Light break into rainbow colors, going into each one of us and giving us exactly what we need at this time. We ask that this Light go five hundred feet above, five hundred feet below, five hundred feet all the way around, and we give thanks for its presence."

As the group came to a close, Dr. Pierce always expressed gratitude for the presence of the Light. Then Light was reaffirmed in order to protect each person when he departed. This was necessary because the chakras and their centers become more vulnerable during prayer and Light work. Closure with protection was always necessary. One closing prayer was: "May we walk in Light. May we become one with the Light. And may the peace and the joy of the Spirit be with us now and always."

At the end of the meeting in order to dissipate the energies in the room, a bell, drum, or bowl was struck three times. Then everyone clapped three times while chanting, "Shanti! Shanti! Shanti!" (translated as Peace! Peace!

Peace!). And after Dr. Pierce met Ogamisama, the **Na-myo-ho-ren-ge-kyo**s were added to the chant.

During the years that the groups took place, there was a great emphasis by Dr. Pierce on encouraging thinking, responsibility, leadership and character building. She would often ask people what they were thinking or what they were experiencing, and she would spontaneously designate individuals to lead the group, to do healing or to say the prayer of protection. For those participating in the group, discomfort was often felt, but character was developed.

MEDITATION

The following meditation prayers spoken by Dr. Pierce emphasize the importance of coming together as a community.

I

Dr. P: We come together in a community of understanding. We come together in a community of striving. We come together in a community of friendship. We ask for awareness and we ask for God consciousness. We ask that the White Light of the Universal Consciousness come and cleanse, purify, and completely protect each of us, that the Light go through, that the Golden Light neutralize and protect the house, under the house, over the house, through the house, into the ground 50 feet, and that a Wall of

Flame completely surround the property. Now we ask that anything that is to be done tonight come into our minds, and that we do it with humility and with love. (**Na-myo-ho-ren-ge-kyo** is chanted several times.)

II

Dr. P: We come together in a community of awareness. We ask for peace. We ask for God Consciousness, and we ask for discrimination tonight to be aware of what is to be done, and we ask that whatever is necessary come into our consciousness. We ask that the White Light of Universal Consciousness come into this room, cleansing, purifying and completely neutralizing any negativity. We ask that it go through both of us, neutralizing anything that is in our bodies that is not normal to these bodies, or anything that will be a detriment. At this time, we ask that this house be completely cleansed and that the Light of the Christ Consciousness go through this room, into the basement, into the office, completely cleansing and neutralizing any negativity and any vibrations that have come in during the day. Now we ask that this house be surrounded with a Wall of Living Flame, and that it go 50 feet into the ground and 50 feet above it, sending a canopy of Living Flame completely over this house, protecting it and sending it down into the ground, cleansing the ground under the house and around it and wrapping it in a Flame of Living Light. And we ask that this property be protected and cleansed, going around to the back of the house, and enclosing the whole in Light. Now, as we start this work, we ask that we be protected in all ways and that we be given the protection that is needed.

III

Dr. P: We come together in a community of understanding. We come together in a community of friendship. We ask for peace; we ask for the presence of the Golden Light of Knowledge and Wisdom. And at this time, we ask for the White Light of the Universal Consciousness to come in, blessing and cleansing, going through the two of us, dedicating us for the work we are to do tonight. And we dedicate this work to the best of our ability, and to the fullest knowledge in every way that is best for those concerned. Now we ask that the Flame of the Christ Consciousness protect this house, that it go 50 feet into the ground completely surrounding this house with a Wall of Living Flame so that nothing that is negative can enter and anything that passes through this Wall of Flame, if it is negative, it will be neutralized or destroyed. We ask that a Wall of Living Flame be placed completely around the property and that anything that passes through it will be cleansed of negativity. We ask that C's tiredness be taken away at this time, and that the Power go through her so that she may see, and I may have the wisdom to ask and have the right answers and have the power to do this tonight. And now in the name of the Christ Consciousness and the Holy Om, we begin this session. (A bell or gong is rung three times.)

And this morning, as we expand our center of consciousness out into space, have it encompass everything that is needed for growth and for understanding. Particularly, have it bring in everything that is needed for now. Expand your consciousness out into space, taking in all of San Francisco and the Bay. Now expand it clear down the Peninsula and take in everything of the Peninsula. Now expand it taking in everything of the South Pacific and the Orient. Now expand it into everything that is in the Western Hemisphere. Now expand your consciousness out to infinity, and know that around you is a force field that brings into you whatever is necessary for you. And as this force field touches and draws into you the thing that sustains you, the thing that gives you power, the thing that gives you knowledge, know that you are a part of it, and that whatever is needed will come to you. So if you will, each day go within your center of consciousness which usually is the area of the heart center. Create your own center and bring into it whatever is necessary for your growth.

C: (says the Lord's Prayer)

Dr. P: (closing) May the Light shine within you. May you become one with the Light. May we become a Light to those with whom we work and those with whom we come in contact each day. May the Light shine through you. May the Light shine about you. And may the Peace of the Spirit be with you now and always. Shanti! Shanti! Shanti! (**Na-myo-ho-ren-ge-kyo** is chanted several times.)

IV

"We come together in a community of striving, a community of understanding, a community of peace. We ask for awareness and we ask for God Consciousness, and we ask that the Light of the Christ Consciousness come into this room purifying, revitalizing, and completely cleansing this room and both of us. We ask that the Light go through this house, releasing any negativity and anything that is not for the best of anyone who enters.

"This morning we build a castle of Light to the East. We build it as a temple, and the steps of this temple of White Light are a lovely green-gold light that lead into a deep amphitheater which is blue, with a faint of green and of purple, all of this light being concentrated as it comes in. And at the end where the altar is, there is a pillar of White Light. A lady in White Light gives to anyone who comes into this temple a touch of Universal Consciousness.

"We build a spire of White Light that leads toward the sun, and this spire leads out into a thin thin shimmer that goes off into space until it connects and brings into this temple of Light the colors of the rainbow and whatever is needed.

"To the East, we build this temple, and today we go toward the sun and become one with the Light and one with the sun within the temple. As we go up the steps into the amphitheater, we feel these rays of peace coming down and through the temple.

"Now we move to the North. We make a complete temple of White Light. We create this temple in which people can be taken for revitalization and renewal. We can take them there when it is needed, and we create this to be a permanent substance to the North where it will stay.

"We construct a temple to the South that is stately and is filled with the direct Light of the sun and is filled with a warm golden Light from the warmth of the Spirit and the pink from the heart. This temple is a special one where the Light is abundant, and any persons entering there will be warmed by the Light of the sun and the Light will be tempered according to their needs. They will go in and be bathed by the warmth, be surrounded and permeated by the warmth of the sun and the warmth of Light which penetrate outward. This is available to anyone who passes through.

"To the West we place a temple where the sun crosses. And this temple is especially protected and given to those who need strength at the end of the day, a special time when some people feel weary, and before they retire. This temple is large and strong and filled with all the reflections of the rays of the setting sun. There is a beautiful view. There is pink for love, and rose for emotional healing and attunement of the Spirit that reaches anyone through the reflection of the rainbow and the path of the setting sun. This will especially be used by the Spirit, and for sustenance for the body that is weary at eventide, and for the Peace of the Spirit and Peace in the Heart. Each temple at eventide is one of peace and stability and is there for anyone who passes nearby and wishes to enter.

"We connect these temples of Light with the rainbow colors going out to the East, to the North, to the West, and to the South. We connect them with the center of Light that is in this room."

Chapter VI

THE AURIC FIELD

"Negative thoughts sear the aura."

—Gayle C. Pierce

THE AURA

"The auric field is a representation of our physical living energy and an emanation of our life force. It is a magnetic field created by the body. It comes from within the body and extends outward. When you put your hands together and begin to pull them one to two feet apart, you may see white threads coming from the hands. Then the threads disappear. When this energy goes from your hands, it is like a white substance. This is actually *prana* that you are sending to the patient. It will go into that patient and fill him until he has as much as he can take, and then the power will stop flowing through your hands. It is a definite force. We give this vital force when we cleanse or heal. When some people sense the area of need, energy immediately goes through their hands. The energy from the hand flows differently with different people. Because the aura of the hand extends way out, it is different from other parts of the body. In a highly evolved person the energy has fluorescence. A person's health, including illness, disease, and trauma are seen as colors in the aura.

"When human relationships are in discord, cords may be formed that attach themselves to the individual. These cords both weaken the auric field and the person's overall abilities, including his emotions and his health. They must be cut, neutralized, and detached from the person and the situation. It is necessary to state that the attached cords are cut, neutralized, and returned to both the source and the affected person. The person affected must be willing to have the emotional cords that he has sent out to others neutralized and returned to him. This enables him to regain stability in thought and energy. The colors most appropriate for his healing are then brought into the aura.

1. Cleansing

"Because the auric field is magnetic energy, we absorb things (emotions, thoughts, energy) from other people. When working with people it is important to wear something that will allow the outflow of negative energy which will also reduce nerve tension. We build up terrific force and negative tension which is the negative electricity of the body. Shoes with rubber soles are particularly poor for this reason since rubber inhibits the outflow of energy. It is good to go without shoes for a portion of time in order to release negative energy.

"Always begin cleansing with the White Light as this is for your protection. When checking a patient for healing, you must feel, be, and get a sense of the patient without attachment. What you have in your mind and the intensity with which you apply your concentration is how much the patient gets out of the healing. Complete concentration and impersonal love are needed.

"Cleanse the patient's auric field by making sweeping motions down the body to take out negativity. It is important to clean out the auric field in order to get vital force to the patient. Focus on the arms and legs. Place your left hand on the base of the skull and your right hand over the solar plexus, sending knowledge, love, approval, and understanding. When a person lets out a big sigh, you know that what you have given has been received."

2. Healing

For healing to be effective, the healer must be emotionally detached from both the person and the outcome.

"Using one hand for healing serves the purpose of sensing better. One hand brings in the power (palm up) while the other (palm down) transmits it. Sometimes you can really feel a hot spot (a specific area in need of healing). It may be that you have already begun to transmit to the need of the patient, and the response is a pulling motion. Many times this will happen before you clearly detect the area of need. You can postulate that any negativity or anything that is not normal to the body be released. After cleansing the auric field, the White Light (tempered) is sent through the body from the top of the head to the tips of the toes. The person being healed can also visualize this White Light within himself. Then the White Light that has been tempered according to the person's needs is sent down through the center of the forehead to neutralize all negativity and to heal every cell in the body. Every cell has a life force and it is a unity in itself. Send the Light to every cell for wisdom and understanding in order to revitalize energy in all the cells. Then bring the rose-red light of love into the heart center. Send it out with every beat of the heart, love to every cell for revitalizing and restoring every cell in the body, and giving whatever is necessary. This includes the long bones. People who are rational and mental tend to think intellectually with their heads. They need to bring energy from the heart center, the center of compassion, and from the solar plexus, the center of emotions, in order to activate their heart centers.

3. Dimensions of the Aura

"The auric field comes out farther around the head and shoulders. It is about two inches outside of and along the body, but on a very vital person it comes out to about four inches. There is a subtle difference between the aura of the body and the aura of the head. When using the White Light to examine the auric field, consciously be aware of sending this Light into the areas that need healing. In a skull fracture, for example, there may be a terrific pulling in of energy which is unusual, as the energy usually goes out from the head. When healing, do not miss the head. When the pituitary and pineal glands are involved there will be a feeling of coolness at the center on the top of the head and at the center of each eyebrow. These are the reflex points for the pituitary. The pituitary is the area where the vital force first comes in as a cone of Light and channels into the thymus and downward to the spleen. These spiritual centers (chakras) are spiritual energy centers in the body that work through the endocrine glands but are not limited by them. If the glands or organs are gone (surgically removed or damaged), or not functioning properly, the energy vortex is still present and still usable. Sending Light into a jagged tear in the aura is difficult. It feels like you are just pouring energy in but losing it. This tear is more than just a bump as it usually involves a trauma or accident. These healing techniques are to be used carefully because healing affects the vital part of the human mechanism.

4. Scanning the Aura

"The palms of your hands must be turned downward when making passing motions over the body at a distance of a half-inch above it. You can also use passing motions a half-inch away from a tree, an animal or a flower in order to feel their vibrations.

"I use both hands when I go over the auric field, and usually one hand follows the other. As energy and power come out of your hand, the person is given a certain amount of energy. Then we have the person turn over and lie face down. Usually when you pick up an area of need in the solar plexus, you pick up an emotion that is either present or past. You can key into something that happened some time ago, and it can be just as accurate as if it were in the present time. Follow the energy field (emanations) of the body. This field is an oval shape that encloses the whole individual. It is termed the auric egg. This auric field is very close to the body if the vitality is low.

"It is very important for a slapping motion to be done on long bones to start new patterns for red blood cells and to get energy into the body. The slapping is a firm tapping with the index, middle, and ring fingers along the sternum (heart center) at the head of the ribs. This is particularly important when electrical shock causes limitation in movement or damage to the brain. When bone marrow is involved, I project White Light and right action to completely clear up the situation. When a spleen is removed, the life span is shortened and doctors do not know how to look at this in terms of vital force. This information is what is called 'hidden knowledge,' which is passed from person to person."

'Hidden knowledge' consists of teachings that are passed orally from teacher to student.

"A quick scan of the body is often most effective as first impressions are often correct. If you take too long, the mind gets cluttered. Use the hand to scan the body and watch for any temperature drop (fluctuation), or tingling in your hand. If you feel as though you get a handful of energy when doing the healing, then throw it off by shaking the hands. Then wash your hands, including above your wrists, in cold water. Old thought forms can be taken out permanently from the force field with this technique of cleansing.

5. A Break in the Auric Field

"It is unusual for the auric field to be broken and it must be caused by a shock, either an emotional or a physical one. It can also happen if a person overextends himself. If you were to get a shock in your hand, the auric field around the entire arm could be broken. If you hit your head, the break in the auric field will be on the opposite side of the brain. This is because the brain is suspended in water and when the head is bumped, the brain is thrown in the opposite direction. So the cause of the break can come from either outside or inside the body. A bump on the top of the head puts pressure on the brainstem. This does not usually happen in the rest of the body.

6. Our Force Field

"Thoughts are things that go out as thought forms in our force field. The force field surrounds you. It is a force power that is around you and that attracts people to you. It is comprised of all your thoughts, your actions, everything that you are and everything that has happened to you. When you put your hands on someone, what you think goes into the psyche of the person you are working on; *this is why you cannot afford to be sloppy in thought. You have to keep your concentration.*

"A shattered force field can be detected when a person is feeling that things are not quite coming together or that what is wrong is not known. The force field will in time re-establish itself with the re-establishment of the aura. If it is left shattered, the person will feel scattered and the flow of energy will be interrupted. Regardless of how much energy you are bringing in, if you are feeling scattered and losing energy, you may have a break in the aura. The person should be checked. We usually do not find it for ourselves. It is very difficult to do for one's self. We can go over our aura and look for the cold spots just as we would do for others. When any one of the spiritual bodies is out of balance it causes trouble for the individual, especially if the centers (chakras) are disturbed from shock, negative environments, or entities. We close these centers from the back which are located up and down the spine.

"To protect your force field and your auric field, Tibetan Buddhism, in fact all Buddhist philosophy and other religious teachings, tell you to walk and speak gently with no quick harsh movements.

WHAT YOU CAN AND CANNOT DO

"Places should be cleansed as well as bodies and auras to free any negativity or any spirits that may be caught. You need to protect yourself and be sure that nothing attaches itself to you. **You can send Light, and that is all you can do until you know you have the power to handle whatever situation may arise.** You have to be aware of where the person is. You cannot use these methods for healing everyone. This knowledge is a gift of the Spirit, and you do not put a gift of the Spirit before someone who is not ready.

PSYCHIC ATTACK

"Weaknesses or rents in the aura leave a person open to psychic attacks and to negative emotions. A person may also have, through his own negative thoughts, created an elemental, a form energized and empowered by repetitious thoughts. The cutting of the cords followed by the bringing in of Light to cleanse, purify, and fill the weakened aura can give a person an opportunity to heal on the physical, mental and spiritual levels. A disorder in a person may become an obstacle that inhibits spiritual evolution.

"Trauma, nervousness, ongoing stress, and chronic diseases impair the aura by weakening the individual's energy. These rents in the aura open a person to psychic attack and to destructive emotions coming from others. The emotion of anger is destructive for the person sending it as well as for the person receiving it."

Dr. Pierce used the rainbow colors of Light to fill weakened areas of the auric field. She directed to the person the specific colors most needed.

" When a person experiences a psychic attack, his will and volition are usually affected. There can be a loss of interest in spiritual and healing pursuits. Dizziness, illness, fatigue, weakened cognition, and skin disorders are some of the problems that may occur. If an entity is involved, it may be necessary to cast out that spirit. Before casting out any negative force, total and complete protection is absolutely essential. A casting out command may be stated as, 'In the name of Jesus Christ, I demand that you leave (individual's name).' If the entity refuses, the demand is stated once again. 'In the name of God, and in the name of Jesus Christ, I demand that you leave (name).' If the entity still refuses to leave, it is mandatory to make a third demand. Each time the demand is stated, it must reflect continued and increased strength, conviction, and power. The tone of voice must be strong, firm, and commanding. A dagger of Light is a useful form to be thrown out to inhibit the entity attacking."

> *Dr. Pierce trained few people in the capacity of working with psychic attacks. She reiterated that working with negative entities is dangerous; therefore, training is necessary and complete protection should be maintained at all times while working with the psychic world. Even with protection and the support of another person or persons, the individual who is casting out may still be adversely affected.*

People who have attempted to do this work without sufficient knowledge and strong protection have been impaired both physically and mentally.

Chapter VII

HEALING

"Your power lies within you."

—Gayle C. Pierce

It is imperative to ask that the White Light surround the person doing the healing so that he or she can perceive and speak clearly.

All persons to be worked with must be asked if they are willing to step into the Light. If they are not willing, thank them, and release them.

Dr. Pierce received many requests for healing. The following examples demonstrate her responses to these requests.

MALE ON THE OTHER SIDE

Dr. P: We ask that (person's name) step into the Light if he is willing. We ask that his guardian angel bring him in and give him protection.

Dr. P (To C): Please look and see what (person's name) is doing. We are to ask if there is anything to do about this, or if we are to leave it alone. We ask that the Flame of the Spirit go through him. We ask that you leave with love, understanding, and with Power. Good night (person's name). Go in love. We put the White Light and the Light of the Universal Power and Consciousness around you.

We were to leave this situation alone.

LIVING FEMALE   (remote healing)

C: I ask that Mrs. (name) come into the Light.

Dr. P: We ask that the Light go through (person's name), that the Golden Light of Ogamisama and the White Light of Universal Consciousness bring health and understanding. This White Light, which is a life-giving ray and the force of life is clear, and it needs to be tempered for the individual.

C: I am not to do anything here. She is better since last week and nothing needs to be done.

Dr. P: We release her with the Peace of the Spirit.

A MOTHER WHO HAS BEEN ON THE OTHER SIDE FOR ABOUT FORTY YEARS

C: I ask permission to see the mother (state complete name), and I ask that those that are with her come also.

She is better and stronger, and there are two beings around her.

Dr. P: We ask that the Light of Understanding and the White Light of Cleansing and the Power go into the mother, and that the Gold Light of Healing and Wisdom be around her so that she can see and hear the things that are necessary for her growth, and in doing so, that she may have a sense of well-being. We ask that any despair, resentment, or grief be taken from her so that her growth may be fast and sure. And let her rest, assured that her family is taken care of here. We ask that she release any earth ties, if she has them, so that she can go forward in love, knowing that there is growth always of the Spirit and growth of understanding. Let her rest in peace, and we ask for her the intense peace of the Spirit and complete rest and quick recovery.

Knowing that you are one with the Eternal Power, and knowing that within you is the Light of your world, and knowing that within each one is the Golden Light of the God Power, let the Healing Ray and the Golden Ray go through your body, transmuting, cleansing, and healing the whole of your body. Let this power of the Spirit, which is the power of the individual, pass through you with healing and with understanding, bringing up anything that is necessary for you to look at, anything that is necessary for you to heal and anything that is necessary for you to know. Tonight we ask your guardian angel to be aware of what you need and to be with you in this week to come.

C: I now ask that those helpers who are with (mother's name), that they help to bring her into the Light so that if there is any more assistance that she needs from this earth plane that we be able to give it to her.

C: I get nothing.

Dr. P: Ask her if she has gone on to a higher consciousness.

C: I ask if (person's name) mother has gone on to a higher consciousness, and if this is the reason I do not get an impression or see anything.

Dr. P: We ask that the mother's angel come and give us information that is about the mother.

C: A being comes and says not to misinterpret the darkness, that she is going on to a higher plane, that she has not gone yet. The guardian angel says that she cannot be seen tonight but to look in at another time.

C: Thank you very much, guardian angel. We send you both love and Light, and I ask that her mother be surrounded in Light and helped to go on to the higher plane. We send you peace and love tonight. Go in peace.

(C tells Dr. P that it seemed like a camouflage, but Dr. P says that there is something going on and that the mother couldn't come, but that the right to ask is always there).

LIVING PERSON—A FATHER (remote healing)

C: I now ask that (person's name) father, (father's name), step into the Light.

Dr. P: And what do you see?

C: Are you aware of your angel since we met last week?

Dr. P (to C): Contact the guardian angel.

C: Will the guardian angel of (person's name) father step into the Light now? The angel says that sometimes he is aware, and sometimes not.

Dr. P (to guardian angel): Do things for him now that you have been contacted.

Dr. P (to C): Ask that the guardian angel do things for the father, to help and give him comfort, and that a little bit of his being aware of his angel is better than nothing at all.

C: I asked the angel what he needed, and the angel said vitamins, specifically Vitamin E. His angel was wearing a yarmulke (Hebrew cap) and said his job was difficult. He is about seven feet tall. I asked (person's name) father to step into the Light, and if he was feeling better from last week's work, that I wondered about the work and how he now felt about his daughter. He responded that he is feeling a little bit better about her ways.

C (to the father): I send you lots of the rose-red color of light.

I ask that any of the helpers of the father protect and guide him day and night and in the days to come, and to give him comfort, that if there is anything he needs to look at day or night it comes to him tempered so that he is able to look. Thank you.

Dr. P: Let's ask the White Light of the Universal Consciousness and the Light of the daughter's own God Consciousness to go through her from the top of her head to the tips of her toes, especially through the emotional body, cleansing and purifying the negativity about her father. Let the White Light go through the emotional body and the area of the father's memories in the daughter, taking away the anger, the fear, the desperation, the resentment and the grief. We ask that whatever is necessary come up into her conscious mind to be dealt with and be healed, that the White Light and the Golden Light of the Ogamisama Ray go through the daughter, neutralizing the negativity of her father's memory and bringing to the surface anything that hasn't already come up for healing and understanding.

May the Peace of the Spirit be with you now and always.

We ask that the colors go through the emotions and that these colors cleanse the emotions as they go into the desire body. Then the daughter's conscious mind will be better able to perceive, to cleanse, and to understand these emotions.

LIVING PERSON—SAME FATHER (remote healing)

C: I ask (person's name) father, (father's name), to step into the Light right now. I can see him. The angel says that he is having trouble with the father who doesn't want to see things.

C: I called you in, not because I want you to become involved with your daughter's thoughts, but to call your guardian angel as he needs to be called in, in order to help you. You were not really aware of him before.

C (to angel): I know you have not been called in for a good many years. We thank you.

C: I would like you to see your daughter more objectively.

C: I see that he sees her as his little girl.

Dr. P (to the father): Let her grow up, and come to the age where she is now. She must grow in order for her spiritual growth to become complete, and for her to become a completely functioning human being. Can you release her to be a young woman, a person, and to become the beautiful gracious person that you know your daughter is?

Dr. P (to C): Look at how (person's name) father feels about her, and let him keep his own reality, and his daughter keep hers.

Dr. P (to the father): Mr. (name), your daughter is a beautiful young woman. Try to accept her. Release her and let her be a woman so that she can fulfill her duty and teach children properly, and she will have a better relationship with you. Why don't you release her? If you will accept your guardian angel, he will give you companionship and a lot of direction, and he will help you when you need help, and he will help to take you places. He will accept you in every way, and if you would accept your guardian angel, that would be nice. When we speak to you next week, we will talk about it, but let your daughter be a woman, and let your guardian angel be with you this week. Imagine that there is someone with you at all times. When you need someone, call him. Just pretend and see how real it is. You are doing a beautiful job of adjusting to your life, Mr. (name). Now you go ahead and do the things that you have to do, and this week try to release your daughter to her own reality, and you keep your own. We say good night to you for tonight. We send you Light and love. So good night Mr. (name), and we send the Light and love to surround you for the coming week.

LIVING PERSON—A SISTER (remote healing)

C: I would like (person's name) sister, (sister's name), to step into the Light. Last week she said she thought she could like her sister.

Dr. P: When you start working with people's basic emotions and seeing them the way they really are, then you have to get into this. We ask that the Light go through (sister's name), and the power of the Healing Ray of Ogamisama, the Golden Ray, and the rose-red light of love go through her and give her peace, and heal some of the negativity and bring some of the understanding to her.

C: She thinks metaphysics is hogwash and would like her sister to be like her friends, ordinary in her way of thinking.

Dr. P: Is there anything else she'd like to bring out within herself about her feelings? Can you send the rose-red light to her by visualizing her as a baby and then sending her the Light each year as you see her get older, up to her present age?

C: I ask her Guardian Angel to step into the Light. I noted that the angel had become tired by working with her confusion. We put Light around the angel and around (sister's name) to try to dispel the gray cloud.

Dr. P: We ask that the White Light of God Consciousness come into (sister's name), dispelling this grayness and giving her more awareness of the color of Light. Let the rainbow colors flash through her desire body, and let them come through to such a point that they dispel all grayness and all the lead-like quality that is around her. We ask that she become more aware, and that this Light go forth to her, dispelling, cleansing, and purifying.

We ask that her guardian angel be given the White Light, and that around him shines the Golden Light of Understanding and Warmth. Let him be more aware of her needs, in spite of the fact that she does not see him or is not aware of him.

There is always a child in a human being, and when you send love that can be sent at any time, it goes to the child who feels the warmth of being loved. Send it to the heart center with extreme warmth, extreme concentration, and extreme desire that it reach the person. Knowing this, send it as if she is there and send it at the age she needs it, using your intuition.

C: She needs it very much at one month, up to six months, as there is a lot of grief around her. She doesn't have any of the warmth and the life and the joy that should belong to a baby. From six months to three or four years, she felt love. The only thing I can do is send love to the periods when I felt she needed it, and try to sense what she needs.

Dr. P: Sibling rivalry is always the momentary resentment of each other. Do you feel it is more than this? Send the love. This is the thing you have to do, and this is the thing you can do for her. Let anything that needs to be done next week come into our consciousness. At this time we will ask that the Golden Light of Healing and Understanding pass through her from the top of her head to the tips of her toes, bringing her peace, bringing her energy and understanding of all these massive amounts of material. And may the Peace of the Spirit be with all of us. And we ask that the Peace of the Spirit be with her now and always, and so for tonight, we close this session. **Na-myo-ho-ren-ge-kyo** (chanted several times.)

DIFFICULTY CONCERNING A LIVING SON AND HIS MOTHER WHO HAS PASSED ON BUT MAY BE EARTHBOUND

Dr. P: If it is possible, may we look at (person's name) mother and see if she is earthbound or if there is anything that needs to be done at this time. Let's send her Light and peace and the desire to do whatever is necessary for her own growth, the Growth of the Spirit, and that she be released from any ties of bitterness and resentment because there is deep dark resentment all around her. Let's see if we can throw Light through the resentment and completely encompass her in Light, and the Golden Ray of Ogamisama will help to release this woman.

We ask that the Golden Ray of Ogamisama and the **Na-myo-ho-ren-ge-kyo**s go forth. We ask that the Light go to her to guide her wherever she needs to go for her to have the Growth of the Spirit.

Dr. P to C: There has to be a desire to be released. We can only do what we can in regards to the person who doesn't want or won't make a transition.

Dr. P: For now we must leave the mother in Light with helpers and her own guardian angel. We must ask her guardian angel to be aware and to try and keep the mother in Light, to leave her with the hope that this will be done in order for her to complete her transition. We can look next week. I will look later at the mother.

We release her for this moment of time, and we now go back and see if there is anything more we must do for her son.

Let's surround the son in the Golden Light and the warm red light of love and all of the lovely warm colors of the rainbow, the orange, the soft orange-reds, the pinks, and the warm colors of the spectrum. Let's particularly use the rose-red light of love and the soft pink light of love, which is a higher vibrational quality of spiritual love. Let's surround him entirely and have this soft pink go through him, and let this warmth and this light come through his communication and all of the things that he does. Let this man be aware of the warmth pouring through him so that he is able to give out his love.

We ask that Ogamisama's Light, the Golden Ray, be wrapped around him and that this Golden Ray shine on him and about him. We ask that the Light move down completely through the spinal column, through the legs and the nerves. And we ask that if it can be done, it will be done. The Golden Light of Ogamisama comes through and does this. If this is karmic, we ask that whatever is necessary be done, and we release it to this Golden Light. We take the White Light and send it through this chakra where there is darkness. We then close and seal the chakra door and cleanse it with White Light. We will leave this in the Golden Light until next time and then we will look when we meet again. We release (person's name) into the Light.

DIFFICULTY CONCERNING A LIVING SON AND HIS MOTHER WHO HAS PASSED ON BUT MAY BE EARTHBOUND

Dr. P: If it is possible, may we look at (person's name) mother and see if she is earthbound or if there is anything that needs to be done at this time. Let's send her Light and peace and the desire to do whatever is necessary for her own growth, the Growth of the Spirit, and that she be released from any ties of bitterness and resentment because there is deep dark resentment all around her. Let's see if we can throw Light through the resentment and completely encompass her in Light, and the Golden Ray of Ogamisama will help to release this woman.

We ask that the Golden Ray of Ogamisama and the **Na-myo-ho-ren-ge-kyo**s go forth. We ask that the Light go to her to guide her wherever she needs to go for her to have the Growth of the Spirit.

Dr. P to C: There has to be a desire to be released. We can only do what we can in regards to the person who doesn't want or won't make a transition.

Dr. P: For now we must leave the mother in Light with helpers and her own guardian angel. We must ask her guardian angel to be aware and to try and keep the mother in Light, to leave her with the hope that this will be done in order for her to complete her transition. We can look next week. I will look later at the mother.

We release her for this moment of time, and we now go back and see if there is anything more we must do for her son.

Let's surround the son in the Golden Light and the warm red light of love and all of the lovely warm colors of the rainbow, the orange, the soft orange-reds, the pinks, and the warm colors of the spectrum. Let's particularly use the rose-red light of love and the soft pink light of love, which is a higher vibrational quality of spiritual love. Let's surround him entirely and have this soft pink go through him, and let this warmth and this light come through his communication and all of the things that he does. Let this man be aware of the warmth pouring through him so that he is able to give out his love.

We ask that Ogamisama's Light, the Golden Ray, be wrapped around him and that this Golden Ray shine on him and about him. We ask that the Light move down completely through the spinal column, through the legs and the nerves. And we ask that if it can be done, it will be done. The Golden Light of Ogamisama comes through and does this. If this is karmic, we ask that whatever is necessary be done, and we release it to this Golden Light. We take the White Light and send it through this chakra where there is darkness. We then close and seal the chakra door and cleanse it with White Light. We will leave this in the Golden Light until next time and then we will look when we meet again. We release (person's name) into the Light.

LIVING MALE (remote healing)

Dr. P: We ask that (person's name) step into the Light. We ask that the rose-red light of love go into the heart center and that it completely go through (name's) body, and let it flow with the bloodstream going out to every part of the body so that the body can feel the warmth of the rose-red light of love.

We send the light of love, understanding, and complete awareness pulsing through every part of the body. Let (name) be aware that there is a love in the universe that is more important than any physical or personal love, and let (name) be aware of whatever is necessary for him. Let him be aware of all the love that comes to him from all the people that he knows. Tonight we send the ray of love to him, giving him understanding, peace, a sense of security and awareness.

Dr. P (to C): Shall we send him Light? He is having a bad time.
C: Yes.

Dr. P: We ask that the Light of the Universal Consciousness and the rose-red light of love go to (name), flooding him and giving him energy, understanding, and peace, and we ask that a Wall of Living Flame be around him as protection. We intensify his protection and give him whatever is needed for now, and we send him love in the name of the Christ Consciousness. Thank you.

Dr. P (to living male): Why don't you find someone who will give you what you need? Ask your guardian angel to give you something of love and understanding until you get your own balance and can find someone who can love you for what you are and give you the things you need. Go into the Light and take Light, and become a person of Light. We send you Light tonight. Go in peace and go with God.

Chapter VIII

TRANSITION

"We are all alone in time and space."

—Gayle C. Pierce

PRAYER FOR TRANSITION

"We ask in the name of the Hierarchy of Light, and we ask that you go in understanding and Light. We give thanks.

"We can ask the Living Wall of Flame to be placed around the person.

"Remember to release a person to his own God.

"We ask that anything that is his return to him, that he realizes this is a new experience and that he must walk alone. We ask that the White Light release anything that is not complete.

"Many times when we think of something that is not completed on the earth plane by the person in transition, it will come to that person's consciousness, and something can be done. Place the Cross of the Spirit (Equidistant Cross) on the person's chest, and ask that the Power of the Spirit go through him. Then say to the helpers: we are aware of your help; we thank you; we ask that he be given power and protection. Now, we ask that he be encased in the Armor of Light. We ask that the Flame of the Spirit flow into the body to cleanse, renew, and take care of anything that has been contaminated. We ask the healers and the helpers, and those on the other side who are helping the person in transition, to protect and take care of (name).

"The healers can come to either side, particularly to someone who has been ill. They may already have been helping the person who, in passing, goes in and out of consciousness and into another phase. They help heal the person's consciousness of the memory of the illness. It is important to release illness.

"Because time is an indefinite factor, the soul may go out a long time before the body dies, particularly when the mind is affected. The ill person's soul may go out and come back. In people who have vegetated, the soul goes out, but the cord may not be severed. For others who are around, and who need help in transition, we ask them to go to the Light."

It is important to remember to protect yourself before praying for others. This is the purpose of the prayers of protection.

Prior to prayer work, ask that Angels of Light come into the room to guard and to protect each corner of the room as well as its occupants.

Dr. Pierce often spoke of the silver cord that is the connecting cord of the soul to the body. As death approaches the silver cord is loosened and eventually severed. When the cord is severed the soul is released from the body.

INDIVIDUAL TRANSITIONS

PERSON I

(Confusion regarding transition)

Dr. P: We ask that those beings tending (name) help us so that we may now see how (name) is progressing, and if any help is needed at this time. We ask that (name) be seen in the Light.

C: The person is confused and doesn't know what to do.

Dr. P: (Name), we ask that you look at or feel your way toward Light, and be aware that there is Light somewhere near you and that you go in that direction. There will be someone to help you who will give you the Light that you need so that you are no longer confused, and these beings will give you direction.

C: We ask that the Angels of Light guard and keep him, give him whatever he needs to know for his understanding, guide him at this time, and give him protection.

C: Is told to check back again when (name) gets used to the Light.

Dr. P: Thank you for your assistance.

PERSON II

(Does not know what to do on the other side)

C: We now ask that we are able to help (name), and we ask those beings that are with him, help him step into the Light so that we know if there is anything more that he needs at this time. If so, we want to do it for him.

C: The person on the other side states that he does not know what to do.

Dr. P (to C): Send him more Light.

C: We ask that the Angels of Light encompass Light totally around him, and that he is completely filled with Light, and we give him understanding. We ask that the colors that (name) loved and knew so well be completely enfolded around and about him, and above and below so that he is enveloped in the colors which are most desirable and needed by him at this time.

Dr. P: We ask that the Light of the Spirit enfold (name). We ask that the Angels come near him, bringing their Light, their warmth, and their comfort, bringing the peace of their understanding around him, and the softness of the scintillating colors of their wings and their vibrations.

Dr. P (to person): We ask that you become aware of these. We ask that you let the White Light of the Universal Understanding go through you. Let it go completely through you, around and about you, and let the Gold Light of the Christ Consciousness envelop you and keep you. We leave you until the next time, and we will watch you and look in from time to time to see how you are. Now we leave you with peace, with joy, and with understanding.

And thank you, Angels of Light, for participating.

PERSON III

(Need for support and comfort in transition)

Dr. P: We ask that the White Light of the Universal Consciousness go through (name), and we ask that the Gold Light of Ogamisama's ray penetrate and go into (name). We ask that the rainbow colors go into him and give him the things that are necessary for his state of consciousness, and whatever is necessary at this moment in time, we ask that it be given to (name).

We ask that the Hierarchy of Knowledge or whoever helps the soul be with (name), and that whatever is needed be given for the growth of the Spirit. We ask that the earth cords be severed, so that (name) might go on his way, and we ask that (name's) wife be given comfort and peace, and let her be aware of the completeness of transition, and let her know that it is alright, that it is a natural thing. Let her have comfort and rest and peace. Let her have comfort that (name) is gone, and that he is not clinging to a memory. Know that the reality of death is only like opening a door. We ask that the healing be done, that (name) be at peace, and we leave this at this time for two weeks, and for now it is finished.

PERSON IV

(Releasing fear in transition)

Dr. P: We ask that (name's) desire body be here, and we ask to see the reason for her fear. We ask to know why this fear is around her, and we ask that the power and understanding go through her so that she has peace of mind. Whatever condition is holding her down, she can go on and she can ask for Jesus. We ask that the guardian angel minister to the husband and the son, and to help them be aware of their angels.

PERSON V

(Doing well on the other side)

Dr. P: We ask that the Angel of Light bring (name). We ask that the Light go through his feet and that the Light go all around him. We thank those who have come to do the work. We place him in the care of his guardian angel. You, (name), go into this beautiful garden, this garden of Light, love, and understanding to bring out your beautiful plants of the Spirit. (This is in response to his saying that he is going to be doing something with plants.) So, good night and God bless you.

PERSON VI

(Man with little awareness of his emotions before passing on)

Many times when someone who is on the other side is asked to be seen by a person on the earth plane, there are two or more helpers with him. This is because the person on the other side needs a great deal of help to get from one side to the other.

Dr. P: We ask you to come into the Light, and we ask your guardian angels, and the Angels of Light, to bring you in to see if there is something further we need to do for you. We ask that the Archangel Raphael come and work with my healing angel. Please help this man, Raphael, to adapt and to adjust to his new circumstances. Let him be aware of where he is and of the fact that he must grow spiritually. We send the desire and the Light to do this. We ask that his guardian angel know what to do and stay with him at all times. But Raphael, will you please take him in the shelter of your wings and give him Light? We ask this in the name of the Spirit, and we release him at this time to your healing mission, and to your healing service which we know is much more than we can do. At this time we release (name), and we will check in a couple of weeks to see if there is anything more that we can do. Will you please let us know at that time? Thank you, Archangel Raphael, for your beautiful lovely purple ray that you have brought into the room. Good night.

PERSON VII

(Male who recently passed on; no helpers seen;
he is experiencing difficulty in making his transition.)

Dr. P: If it is necessary, we ask that the helpers from the other side bring you in, and that we be shown what is needed to be done to help you at this time. We ask that all ties, including all earth ties, be severed from (name). We take a pair of golden scissors and cut all ties that bind him to earth, and we ask that the Light go through him.

We ask that the Light of the Spirit go through you, (name), and fill you and make you whole, and that you become aware that you have a spiritual heritage, and that within you can be the power, the knowledge, and the Light for your world, that you are a part of a God Consciousness and a plan for growth. Let it fill you with understanding, with Light, and with power, and we ask that the Light come to you now and that you accept help from the helpers on the other side.

As you go toward the Light, the Light comes toward you, but the decision is yours. You must ask for help and go toward the Light. The power is there, and the understanding for you is there, and the way to growth is there. Walk toward the Path of Light, walk toward the path of peace, walk toward the path of growth, and it will welcome you and give you peace. (Man begins to walk in the direction of the Light).

Until he makes the contact, we ask that (name's) guardian angels stay with him awhile longer. We release him now to go toward his path and to go toward the Light.

Dr. Pierce said that when a person walks toward the Light, the Light comes to the person. We can only make the contact. The person has to do the work for himself.

C: We ask for the Angels of Light and the colors that (name) so loved in his lifetime to be around him, and that he is protected with energy, health, and knowledge.

Dr. P: A person on the other side has to be aware that he has control over his body. He must realize in his thinking that there is no illness and that this thought is the controlling factor. Suddenly, one day he will realize that the way he had thought isn't the way it is at all, and he will move forward. But until this is realized, the body has to be handled like a physical body so that there is no shock.

Dr. Pierce also said that it is important to tell the person that there is no sickness on the other side, and that if he can realize he is well, he will be well. If the person can't realize wellness, he can pretend that he is well, and he will soon be well.

We have to be taught that we are not body, but Spirit, so that when we go over to the other side, we can handle it. It is just a transition, and we must be ready for another life. We must be ready for this transition.

PERSON VIII

(Disturbance)

The following opening prayer is the preliminary step of individual protection necessary before assisting the person who is disturbed in transition.

Dr. P: We ask at this time that the protection and the Wall of Living Flame be reinforced around the house, and reinforced around us, so that nothing can enter and we are completely encompassed with this Flame of the Spirit. It is a protection against any negativity.

We ask that if (name) will step into the Light, we can see what is bothering her.

Chapter IX

ANGELS

"We are one with God."

—Gayle C. Pierce

Dr. Pierce worked primarily with the archangels Gabriel, Michael, Raphael, and Uriel, each of whom emanates from one of the four directions.

GABRIEL

In charge of soldier angels and revelation; active in the West for stronger powers of intuition and psychic gifts; patron of communications; spirit of truth and prince of justice; governor of the West; associated with the white ray. Call on Gabriel in the West for stronger powers of intuition and psychic gifts.

MICHAEL

Considered to be the foremost of the seven archangels; leader of the forces of heaven in overcoming the powers of hell; protection; in charge of nature; angel of mercy; governor of the North; associated with the blue ray. Call on Michael in the North for daily protection and for empowerment and motivation in work.

RAPHAEL

Associated with cultures having to do with the improvement of the human race; angel of healing and angel of humanity; master of healing the earth; governor of the South; associated with the green ray. Call on Raphael in the South for healing of body and soul.

URIEL

Rules over universal cosmic consciousness, enlightenment, and insights; teaches the path of the heart and the fire of pure love; helps to turn the worst disappointments into the greatest blessings; governor of the East; associated with the purple and gold ray flecked with ruby. Call on Uriel in the East to help with change.

"Angels cannot work unless asked. Their growth goes along with ours. If someone asks for help, we can call on the angels. We can also ask the guardian angels to assist and guard anything that negatively touches us so that it will always be for our highest good. We all have the right to ask for angels.

If we do not let our guardian angels help us, all they can do is stand by and take on the quality that we have, because their growth is parallel to ours. Angels take on the quality of the persons they are with; we can send colors and Light to them."

Dr. Pierce frequently worked with two specific angels during the last decade of her life. The first was the White Angel who spoke to Dr. Pierce from a point on the right side of her head, behind her ear. Before this Angel could enter the room, Dr. Pierce brought in White Light to clear away any limiting vibrations. The White Angel's presence increased the vibration and the intensity of the Light. This Angel, through Dr. Pierce, conveyed spiritual teachings and insights, and information to people regarding their personal, physical, and daily life concerns.

The information given by the Blue Angel was generalized and universal, usually of a spiritual nature, and at a different vibratory level than that brought by the White Angel. This Angel conveyed spiritual teachings to the group as a whole. Weeks and months could pass without an appearance or a message. The Blue Angel's presence intensified spiritual healing as it was being done for others.

A tone of excitement was noted in Dr. Pierce's voice when she detected the presence of either angel. When Dr. Pierce announced an angel's presence it was apparent that the energy in the room had intensified. It is thought that these two angels were appointed to assist Dr. Pierce in bringing in a higher spiritual consciousness, and to aid the individuals present in achieving their life goals and attaining spiritual growth.

Chapter X

COLOR

"Be aware of your oneness with Light and with Universal Consciousness."

—Gayle C. Pierce

When directing colors to an individual for healing, it is important to use those that most meet the specific needs of the individual. Each color varies in wave length and has its own vibratory frequency. Meanings of color and their uses may *vary.*

Dr. Pierce frequently used colors for healing.

The following is a list of colors and their application:

Blue: spiritual understanding, soothing and comforting

Royal Blue: good judgment, honesty, loyalty, brings balance between the spiritual and the material

Heavenly Blue: steadfastness, hope, faith, healing

Cobalt Blue: awareness and spiritual consciousness

Electric Blue: nervous system and brain

Buttercup Gold: color of the Christ Consciousness

Gold: Light of understanding, knowledge, wisdom, inspiration, healing. Golden Light may be used to neutralize a situation. Use Gold Light for a person in transition.

Yellow: brings health of body, mind, and soul; relaxation, intelligence, and artistic ability; lifts vibrations, increases mental capacity, represents harmony

Lemon-Yellow: strength of mind, artistic thought, color of health

Orange: creative ideas and ideals

Yellow-Orange: health aura

Deep Orange: spiritual activity of the soul

Purple: spiritual knowledge, must be used with greater care then any of the other colors. Purple is the color of the power of the spoken word.

Orchid: symbolic of Universal Consciousness, represents holy dreams and aspirations

Lavender: spiritual striving and dedication, holy and healing vibrations, humility

Amethyst (blue-purple): represents accomplishment through the God power within the individual

Green: peace, abundance, new growth, healing, helpful in overcoming fear

Red (crimson): courage, new life, energy, strength, vitality, determination, perseverance

Pink (crimson red and white): love, joyous vibration, key to abundance

Rose-Red (crimson): light of love, can be spread out in the auric field for protection, brings joy, raises the vibration in the home, overcomes spiritual laziness and indifference

Rose Tints: love vibrations that are above the personal plane. The addition of rose to pink or red raises it into the universal love consciousness and brings health, strength, and vitality. The rose tints are highly important because they are the highest vibration of the Love of God that warms, comforts, and neutralizes all hate vibrations.

Rosy-White (combination of rose and white): healing, love, purity, intuition

Rosy-Pink (combination of red and pink): for healing of negative conditions flood with rosy-pink and the love and joy of the Creator.

Rosy-Gold (combination of rose and gold): Divine Love expressed through health, strength, vitality, healing; harmonizes conditions

Rainbow: life, strength, harmony, joy, healing; symbolizes the unfailing promises of God for all who walk in the Light

White: highest of all the healing vibrations; contains all the colors of the spectrum; cleansing, purifying and uplifting; purity, poise, perfection

Crystal White: known as the Triune Ray which is the combination of Love, Life, and Light

Chapter XI

OGAMISAMA

REMINISCENCES OF OGAMISAMA

"One cannot know how much one remembers, or how much one forgets. I do know and remember the pull toward Japan, *Honbu*, and Ogamisama. It was like a powerful magnet, having been built up through the constant prayer for peace, Ogamisama's teachings, and her presence. It became like a mighty magnet drawing me across the Pacific Ocean into the south of Japan.

"From childhood, I had been responsible to society and to others. I had a large practice with many people depending on me as well as many obligations. One was a group that came to my home to study philosophy. These obligations became increasingly unimportant. Only being near Ogamisama seemed to matter.

"Ogamisama had become the center of my spiritual consciousness. I was aware of that when I first met her in California. Going to Japan, spending four months in *Honbu* with the resulting purification of body and a change in my awareness only intensified this condition. My desire to live and stay at *Honbu* increased. I wanted to be near the Teacher. However, Ogamisama told me that I must go home, that I had not yet finished my work. When my work was finished and I was old, I could come to *Honbu* to live and they would take care of me. She said I would live to be an old lady—very old—but at present I must be 'the doctor.' In the end I would be given the gift of sudden death. For this I was very grateful. I began to ask my Japanese friends how old do Japanese consider old. Always they laughed at me like Ogamisama had done. There was never an answer. So, I still work full-time at being 'the doctor,' thinking of the happy first time in Japan.

"On my return home, there were many patients as Ogamisama had said there would be. My world was full and busy. Here, as in *Honbu*, I could feel the power of Ogamisama, the intensity of it pulling me back. It was like an ache and the magnet was there day and night, a steady pull. When I could not resist, I returned to *Honbu* for a time, Ogamisama always sending me back home.

"I have felt the strength of the vibration that gave grace and peace, understanding and an indefinite quality, which I cannot name. It manifests as a glow of power around a person. Many people saw this glow. Those who did not see, felt it. It was an energy seen and felt around great holy people. Christ and Buddha were seen in various shades of golden light. It gives peace and understanding. It has come from holy people down through the ages—a gateway to a higher consciousness, a radiance and a force. It has left its mark on humanity and on the culture of the world. Ogamisama had this magic.

"Japan has always been for me a warm and welcoming country—green trees, green water, a beautiful place. This time it was late December—cold, bleak, barren with trees bare and stark—flurries of snow staying a short time and no friendly white blanket on the ground. I had great difficulty keeping warm. I hurried from Tokyo to *Honbu*, eager to see Ogamisama.

"For the first time, Ogamisama did not see me at once. When she did see me, there was a difference—a withdrawal and an impersonal approach. She was in a new state of awareness, a world of the Spirit. It was easy to see that things of the earth were much less important to her. I had a definite feeling that Ogamisama was going to leave this world. It came like a flash as she walked into the room. As the long days went by, I thought that I had misinterpreted my feelings and decided to go on to India. Then again something happened. The quality of Ogamisama's sermons changed. She repeated again and again as if she was trying to make us remember what she had said and what she had taught, intensifying old truths, repeating, trying to make us see that she had given us what was necessary for growth. There was a new quality in Ogamisama's actions and speeches as if she were in two worlds—the world of today and the world of tomorrow. I waited, not knowing why. Even *Honbu* had a quality of cold breathless stillness. Sometimes snow came. The plum tree carried a white cover and there was a white haze and mist, lovely against the mountains and a large white tinged winter moon at night. I waited and my heart ached.

"Then came the night when Ogamisama, who had talked each afternoon and evening for many years, stopping only when she went to other cities and countries to do *dendo* (to spread the teaching), stopped in the middle of a sermon. Her great heart and mind were getting ready for the transition away into a higher glory, a higher light and power. The Avatar, Ogamisama, the spiritual leader of a people was taken to a dimension of light and glory. By New Year, Ogamisama had become 'The Bride of God'.

"I watched the people come by the thousands on special trains, paying homage and respect to Ogamisama, the spiritual leader, the strong vital mother, the woman humanitarian, the teacher.

"Ogamisama had the ability to be all things to all people. There was great and deep concern, gratitude for having known her, and a love that only a great teacher can draw from thousands of people. The day was cold, grey and cloudy—no warmth any place. Even nature respected the grief.

"I was frozen inside and sick at heart. A part of my life was finished. Gone was the vital voice of Ogamisama and her compassion. The magic she made by just being there, her beautiful hands put together in greeting or one raised to stress a point, gestures of grace. Gone was all this—gone Ogamisama, gone.

"I was aboard a giant British airliner when the tears came, tears that for hours were uncontrollable—tears for the loss of a great teacher, tears for Ogamisama, the woman who became a spiritual force in Japan, tears for one who left a glow of warmth wherever she walked, tears for Ogamisama who took all people regardless of nation to her heart, tears for me, for my personal loss and the personal loss of other people, and tears for a peaceless world. There was concern about my weeping. In Thailand, a doctor came aboard and asked if I were ill and could he help me? How could I tell him it was my heart that was sick?

"Then I remembered the things I had gained—the charm and grace of the Japanese people, friends, and the gift Ogamisama gave me of awareness and her teaching, the powerful prayer, *Honbu* and all it means. Again I looked at Ogamisama, the Avatar and her vital warmth for all the people she touched. So it touched my heart and warmed me. I felt gratitude flow through my body like a flood of light. The tears stopped and I was healed and humbled. Japan remains a land of enchantment. In my dreams Ogamisama smiles."

This article was written by Dr. Pierce in 1967. It was printed in *Voices from Heaven* and published by Tensho-Kotai-Jingu-Kyo in Tabuse, Yamaguchi Prefecture, Japan.

Ogamisama
Tabuse, Yamaguchi Pref.
Japan, 1967

Chapter XII

OM MANI PADMA HUM

Om Mani Padma Hum is an ancient chant that originated in India in the Sanskrit language and spread to Tibet where the pronunciation was changed to Om Mani Peme Hung (ohm mah nee peh may hoong). It is said that all the teachings of the Buddha are contained in this mantra. When spoken aloud, silently, spun on a prayer wheel or in written form, the chant is said to invoke the attention and blessings of **Chenrezig**, the Tibetan Buddhist deity of the embodiment of compassion. A mantra (prayer) is a sacred phrase, word or sound.

The following explanation on the mantra *Om Mani Padma Hum* was presented by a guest at Dr. Pierce's home.

"***Om* is the *Atma*,** unmanifested, beyond form, the All. *Mani* is the jewel in the center of the lotus that is the temple, the petals of the lotus that reside in my heart. God is the jewel in the center of the lotus manifesting in my heart. God is the jewel in the center of the lotus that is my heart. You keep visualizing this, as you chant the **Om Mani Padma Hum** (ohm mah nee pahd may hum). Of all Buddhist chants, **Om Mani Padma Hum** is the one used most often. You start the **Om** at your navel, and it is like you dip a bucket into the center of your reservoir and pull up a huge bucket of ambrosia, and you bring it up your spine and pour it in your heart **(Hum)** and then go down for another bucket.

"As you chant this, you are joined with all those who have said the mantra purely enough when it is pure. In other words, the mantra is a device to tune into another frequency, so pretty soon the mantra goes on just like a breath. You sort of breathe it in, and I believe it to be an absolutely unbeatable technique. Listen. Fall into it. It is a device for centering and for bringing up energy. Remember to bring it up the spine and pour it into the heart. Breathe in on the **Om.** Three or four chants can be done in one breath."

Chapter XIII

AGNI YOGA

> "We ask for awareness and we ask
> for God Consciousness."
>
> —Gayle C. Pierce

Agni Yoga is a synthesis of both Eastern beliefs and Western thought. It serves as a bridge between both the spiritual and the scientific worlds. It is a path of beauty, love, and knowledge (the Divine Triad), analogous to God the Father (knowledge), God the Son (love), and God the Holy Spirit (beauty). Agni Yoga has been referred to as a "living ethic" because it helps the student discover moral and spiritual guideposts to help him govern his life and contribute to the common good of world brotherhood.

Agni refers to the god of fire, the oldest and the most revered god in the Indian Vedas. Fire has been a symbol for the Supreme Reality in different traditions. The unity of knowledge, love and beauty is Light, which is known as God. This Divine Triad appears in all major religions. Agni Yoga teaches that it is necessary to love everything and to have compassion and pity, even with enemies; that it is necessary to find beauty in everything, including art, nature, human relationships, and culture; and that it is necessary to acquire knowledge of one's self and to develop and express a personal relationship with God. These are the principles of Agni Yoga.

Agni Yoga teaches that the evolution of the planetary consciousness is a necessity and that through individual striving it can be attained for mankind. It is not a religion, a philosophy, or a science. It is a synthesis of all yogas, especially Karma, Bhakti, and Raja Yoga. Agni Yoga is a system of universal knowledge to help the individual live in the world as a spiritual being. It affirms the existence of the Hierarchy of Light, and the center of the Heart as the link between the Hierarchy and the far-off worlds.

Interaction in everyday life is a necessity for the individual who follows the Agni Yoga path. It is not a way of isolation or seclusion. Through actions of love and forgiveness the individual brings balance to an unbalanced world. These acts of love, stemming from an open heart, contribute to the work of the Hierarchy and help the individual to become attuned with the Fiery or Cosmic World.

Beyond the physical world, and very different from it, is the subtle or psychic world. The sphere of the Fiery World, with its much finer energy, lies far beyond the subtle world.

The Agni Yoga Society was founded in 1920 by Nicholas Roerich and his wife Helena.

Helena Roerich wrote, "The greatest benefit that we can contribute consists in the broadening of consciousness and the improvement and enrichment of our thinking, which, together with the purification of the heart, strengthens our emanations. And thus, raising our vibrations, we restore the health of all that surrounds us."

AGNI YOGA TERMS

The following terms, though not complete, are pertinent to the subject material of this book:

> **Agni:** god of fire, the oldest and most revered god in the Indian Vedas
>
> **Discrimination:** one of the first demands on the path of true discipleship. It is the discernment of actions, their causes, and the knowledge of which forces are constructive and which forces bring harm.
>
> **Fohat:** subtlest fiery energy; can only be accumulated by a person with a purified heart; light of a special quality that emanates from any surface. Electricity represents the coarsest form of the visible energy of fohat.

Hierarch: master; adept

Hierarchy: a cosmic concept, a cosmic law which is within every individual. This law ensures that any individual seeking spirituality, will receive knowledge and wisdom at each step of development. In the broadest sense, this cosmic law is symbolized by the biblical "Ladder of Jacob" in which the seeker raises himself from earth to heaven rung by rung.

All steps and levels of consciousness are interconnected. This is why the understanding of Hierarchy is vitally important for the spiritual seeker. On the path of spiritual evolution Hierarchy is considered to be the most powerful of all principles leading to the broadening of consciousness. The whole universe exists, is nourished and supported solely by this principle.

Hierarchy of Light: group of enlightened beings who have freed themselves from human existence through the law of rebirth (reincarnation) and who have achieved self-mastery and entered into a higher state of consciousness. This group is also known as the Masters of Hierarchy, the Spiritual Hierarchy, the Masters of Wisdom, and the Elder Brothers. Members include the Masters Morya (El Moria), Kuthumi (Koot Hoomi Lai Singh), Djwhal Khul, Babaji, Mohammed, Buddha and Jesus Christ, all of whom have come in times of crisis for the uplifting of the human race.

These beings are exalted spiritual teachers of humanity. They work ceaselessly for the uplifting of the world, for the unfolding of the Divine Plan, and mankind's turning toward the Light. Their work extends to aspects of planetary life—politics, education, religion, art, psychology, and economics.

The Masters are known collectively as the Great White Brotherhood. The Masters of Hierarchy will eventually move into the physical plane in this, the Age of Aquarius (New Age) to help prepare human consciousness for the appearance of Maitreya, the next world teacher.

Mahatma (Great Soul): an adept; master of the highest order; an exalted being who has attained mastery over the flesh and possesses knowledge and power equal to the stage of his spiritual evolution

The Mahatmas of the Brotherhood include the seven Greatest Spirits who came to earth from the higher planets for the acceleration of our evolution.

Mahatma Letters: these letters, first published in 1923, were written from 1880 to 1884 to A. P. Sinnett by two Eastern Mahatmas of Tibet whom Madame H. P. Blavatsky acknowledged as her teachers and were the inspiration for her *Isis Unveiled* and all three *Secret Doctrines.*

Master: perfected human being

Prana: Life-Principle; the breath of life

Pranayama: suppression and regulation of breath in the yoga practice

Shambhala: a secret physical place where the great masters or mahatmas reside. Rigden Djapo is the ruler of Shambhala. For Buddhists, the path to Shambhala is the path to enlightenment. Those who seek this path will be guided by symbols, signs, and messages.

Chapter XIV

INFLUENTIAL PEOPLE

The following brief biographical sketches describe individuals who had a major influence in Dr. Pierce's life.

ELIZABETH BRUNNER   1910 – 2001

Elizabeth Brunner, a Hungarian artist, traveled to India from Hungary in search of ancient spirituality in 1930 with her mother Elizabeth Sass Brunner, also an artist. Elizabeth expressed her art through paintings of Indian sculpture, landscapes, village life, classic architecture, and particularly, portraits of great teachers, politicians, intellectuals, artists, saints and villagers. She painted numerous portraits, including those of Satyajit Ray, Uday Shanker, Mahatma Gandhi, Rabindranath Tagore – the poet laureate of Bengal, and Jawaharlal Nehru – Prime Minister of India, who bestowed upon her an award for her contribution to Indian culture. Elizabeth resided in New Delhi, India until her transition on May 2, 2001 at the age of ninety. Her artwork has been exhibited in New York, Los Angeles, San Francisco, London, New Delhi, and various other cities around the world.

India captured both Elizabeth and her mother's imagination primarily because of its colorful scenery, ancient culture, and spiritual heritage. Much of Elizabeth Brunner's inspiration came from the teachings of the Buddha. Both Elizabeth and her mother arrived in Santiniketan, India in February 1930, at the invitation of Rabindranath Tagore. Mahatma Gandhi also invited them to visit him in Coonoor, India. Between 1932 and 1935, they traveled around India. Then they traveled around the world, spending two years in Japan. During World War II, the British authorities interned the Brunners. From 1955 to 1958, Elizabeth visited important places of Buddhist pilgrimages. Between 1961 and 1965, the proceeds from her paintings were given to homeless artists.

Elizabeth has been compared to cosmic artists who paint sincerely from intuition. These artists work under inspiration that seems to spring from a spiritual or divine source beyond themselves. As an artist, Elizabeth was able to create a fusion between the mystic vision of her mind and the concrete form of color and line. For her, painting was a sacred mission.

Influential People

Elizabeth Brunner
New Delhi, India
1997

THE DALAI LAMA 1935 –

His Holiness the Dalai Lama, a renowned world figure now in exile, is the spiritual head of the Yellow Hat Sect of Tibetan Buddhism. Until the arrival of the Chinese communist rule in 1959, he was the Tibetan Head of State. There has been a Dalai Lama ever since the Yellow Hat Sect arose in the fourteenth century. This Sect believes that the Dalai Lama is the physical manifestation of the Bodhisattva Avalokiteshvara, also known as Chenrezig, the Tibetan deity of compassion. Chenrezig is the Tibetan translation for Avalokiteshvara. The current Dalai Lama is the fourteenth incarnation of this deity.

Dr. Pierce and the Dalai Lama
Tibetan New Year's Day
Dharamsala, India. 1986

MAX HEINDEL 1865 – 1919

Max Heindel is known as the greatest Western mystic of the twentieth century. He was born in Copenhagen, Denmark in 1865.

In 1903 he moved to New York City. Later, he moved to Los Angeles, began a study of metaphysics and Theosophy, and joined the Theosophical Society of Los Angeles where he served as vice-president from 1904 to 1905.

When Max Heindel realized that people suffered less from physical pain than from hunger of the soul, helping the people of the world became his driving force.

An Elder Brother of the Rosicrucian Order, who later became his teacher, appeared to Max Heindel before he left Germany in 1907. He developed a very close relationship with this spiritual teacher. After being tested by the Rosicrucian Order and found worthy, he was given instructions and teachings by the Elder Brothers. The primary portion of these teachings appeared in his book, ***The Rosicrucian Cosmo-Conception.***

Max Heindel left a legacy of more than fourteen books regarding Rosicrucian philosophy and their mysteries. For ten years, he worked tirelessly, and in that time he completed as many books as an average author would have written in a lifetime.

Influential People

Max Heindel's teachings have spread throughout the world. He was the instrument by which a great movement was inaugurated —to make Christianity a living factor in the land.

Max Heindel

HELENA SHAPOSHNIKOVA ROERICH 1879 – 1955

Helena Roerich, a student of Oriental and esoteric philosophies, was greatly influenced by Theosophy.

In the early 1920s, she authored several books, including some currently untranslated manuscripts. She translated **The Secret Doctrine** by Madame H. P. Blavatsky, an earlier writer, into Russian. In 1920, she met the Envoys or Masters of Shambhala.

From 1920 to 1937, Helena Roerich telepathically, in alliance with El Moria (Master Morya), one of the Masters of Shambhala, wrote thirteen books that are commentaries on the teachings of Agni Yoga. Mrs. Roerich stated that she only transmitted the teachings from Master Morya for the good of humanity. She wrote numerous letters and corresponded with many disciples and spiritual aspirants around the world. A portion of these letters is published in her **Letters of Helena Roerich, Volumes I and II.** She was a passionate champion for women and their achievements.

Helena Shaposhnikova married Nicholas Roerich in St. Petersburg in 1901.

Helena Ivanovna Roerich, 1937

NICHOLAS ROERICH 1874 – 1947

Nicholas Roerich, a man of great breadth and spirituality, left an immense legacy to mankind which includes 7000 paintings, articles, lectures, and thirty books. He was also a philosopher, educator, archaeologist, and peacemaker. He is known worldwide for his paintings that are exhibited in museums throughout the world.

In 1921 in New York City, he created the Master's Institute of United Arts that enabled students to study any and all the arts under one roof. In 1958 in New York City, the Nicholas Roerich Museum was chartered. It remains in operation today.

Because he believed that art would unify all humanity, Nicholas Roerich amassed support for an international treaty to protect and preserve cultural institutions and monuments in times of war. In 1935, the Roerich Pact Treaty was signed in the White House in the presence of many world leaders, including President Franklin D. Roosevelt. Those registered in the Pact could display a distinctive flag designed by Nicholas Roerich, known as the Banner of Peace. This banner is an ancient symbol that has been found in many cultures around the world. It consists of three red spheres surrounded by a red circle on a white field. It has been interpreted as a symbol for the past, present, and future achievements of humanity within the Circle of Eternity.

Nicholas Roerich was not an adherent of any established philosophical or religious movement. His spiritual philosophy incorporated elements of Buddhism, Hinduism, Pantheism, Theosophy, Eastern Orthodoxy, the Theory of Relativity, and Agni Yoga.

In 1947, Nicholas Roerich died in India. A large stone in front of his home bears the inscription: "The body of Maharishi Nicholas Roerich, great friend of India, was cremated on this spot on 30 Mahar in the year 2004 of Vitram era, corresponding to 15 December 1947. OM RAM."

Banner of Peace
Designed by Nicholas Roerich

Nicholas Roerich
United States
1934

OGAMISAMA   1900 – 1967

"Wherever you go, wherever you are, go with God."

She was named Sayo Kitamura but is known by her followers as Ogamisama (the great god). She founded a religion known as Tensho-Kotai-Jingu-Kyo in Tabuse, Yamaguchi Prefecture, Japan. In 1944, "The Prophet of Tabuse, Japan", as she was called, received revelations. Tensho-kotai-Jin, the absolute God of the Universe, descended into her body and instructed her to establish the kingdom of God on earth. Shortly afterwards, she was told to chant **Na-myo-ho-ren-ge-kyo.** Before she began her daily sermons in July 1945, she experienced several years of strict religious austerities.

Ogamisama began to travel throughout Japan in 1944, and from 1952 to 1965 she visited the United States several times. In November 1964 she commenced a nine-month world tour that covered thirty-six countries and ended in July 1965. For twenty-three years, wherever she went, she gave what is considered to be God's message.

She taught that one must purify his soul, heart, and mind to fulfill his purpose, his service to God, and to his fellow man. Her philosophical teachings stressed righteous conduct. She also taught that in finding the path to God, anyone could correct his attitudes and purify himself of hatred, greed, and other emotional excesses. She stated that peace begins in the heart of an individual and spreads to the family, and ultimately to the brotherhood of all nations.

"You will never understand your true duty as a human being on earth as long as you are preoccupied with worldly position, fame, money, property, and social custom. If you can detach yourself from thinking about these things, you will be able to understand the spiritual world.

"People are bound by their past, present, and future karmas which they must bear as they walk along the road of life. Their past karmas will appear in their lives continually. If they accept it humbly and polish their souls, they will be on their way."

When Sayo Kitamura ascended in 1967, her granddaughter Kiyokazu Kitamura (Himegamisama) succeeded her.

Ogamisama
Tabuse, Yamaguchi Prefecture
Japan, 1967

Ogamisama with Dr. Gayle C. Pierce
Tabuse, Yamaguchi Prefecture
Japan 1965

RECOLLECTIONS

"In Dr. Gayle's living room, time stood still and space expanded. I always left her group meditation with a broadened perspective and a deepened connection with the Power of the Spirit. For her dedication to God, her teachings and her love, I am grateful." T. K.

∞

"I would consider Dr. Gayle as the foremost influence in my life. She had her feet of clay which gradually I came to recognize. But there was a God Presence that shone through her that I will never forget. It was this Presence that helped illuminate my defects of character as well as my strengths." R. K.

∞

"Dr. Gayle gave shape to my search for meaning in life. She was there for me, as a guide and a signpost on my personal journey of the Spirit. I saw myself more clearly when I was around her. What more can one ask of another?" N. C.

∞

"I was with Dr. Pierce at her initial meeting with the Dalai Lama on the occasion of the Tibetan New Year in Dharamsala, India in 1986. When Dr. Pierce met the Dalai Lama she immediately started to cry. I was pleasantly surprised to discover how ingenuous and informal the Dalai Lama was. His smile was mischievous while he played with her aluminum cane, but Dr. Pierce could not stop crying.

"She had the knack of being in charge yet welcoming others with graciousness, humor, humility, and penetrating concern. She could be as humble and docile as she was imperious. When asked about her work, she could be very evasive. One famous reply to this question was 'whatever is needed'.

"Dr. Pierce settled on a traditional path of yoga known as Agni Yoga; however, she, by her own actions, pointed out that there are other styles appropriate for each person. One teaching she often repeated to me was 'You know, we are all alone in time and space'.

"Dr. Pierce took great interest in my varied activities, whether it was my work, my relationships, or some issue I had been grappling with.

"To have had a friend such as Dr. Pierce, who embodied the Teachings so colorfully and completely, was both a rare gift and an ongoing special responsibility." P. P.

∞

"I walked up to the interesting, somewhat mysterious stucco house with the colorful stained glass window and rang the doorbell; the door had a very tiny window at eye level that opened from the inside, and two bright blue eyes peered out—my first encounter with Dr. Gayle, with many to follow. She was an utterly fascinating person, combining the characteristics of a wise teacher and a curious child in a totally harmonious way. If you came for a treatment and complained about a pain in your back, she promptly dug her fingers into your intestines or some other unrelated area, and would tell you—now, that is where the problem is. And she was correct!

"During the course of my eighteen years of study with her and our group every Friday night, I benefited from her teachings, healings, personal advice, and love. There were many guests that came to visit her very international house: American Shamans, British writers, Indian gurus, and last but not least, the Tibetans, her very special visitors. There is a great void in my life since her passing and I miss her dearly." E. Z.

∞

"When she said 'I love you,' you knew that she spoke the Heart of God." M. A.

∞

"I first met Dr. Gayle in the early winter of 1981 at her Friday night meditation group. After the Invocation of Light, a protection prayer, meditation, and a few readings from the Agni Yoga books, she asked the twelve of us the purpose of our lives. Floored by the question, I began a seventeen-year journey that would forever imprint her mark on my soul.

Recollections

"Dr. Gayle introduced several of us to the realms of the spiritual, the material, and the world in between which is called the subtle world. She was able to define these worlds, explain the landscape, and provide the experiences to allow one to discover these worlds within oneself. She had the intuitive ability to draw out and affirm one's true inner spiritual nature and support its development. As a triple Leo, she also had the tenacity to let a person's ego know where it really stood. Dr. Gayle's home served as a hub for the inner journeys of patients, friends, healers, teachers, and students of all traditions and spiritual orientations at various stages of healing and development. We often heard Dr. Gayle affirm 'All paths lead to God.' People who met her were touched in a way that few mentors can affect or have the ability to comprehend.

"After Dr. Gayle died, many of her students surrounded her bed and began the prayers she had taught us for a spirit's release from a body, which is typically a seven-week process. Upon arrival at her bedside, it was obvious that Dr. Gayle's spirit had completely left her body. In consultation with a Tibetan lama, Khamtrul Rinpoche, a highly accomplished Nyingma Master in Dharamsala, India, he explained that Dr. Gayle had skipped the Bardo, the intermediate state between death and a new incarnation. For me, she was a very advanced soul; her striving and dedication were for the well-being and spiritual development of those who were fortunate enough to have met her. Blessings to her and her aspirations!" P. T.

∞

"As for all of us, Dr. Gayle has influenced our lives in many ways. She was the bridge into my new single life after the sudden death of my husband." V. M.

∞

"I have enclosed a special letter to Gayle. It is on gold paper for mastery in the heart and for love." D. R. (This letter was presented to Gayle at her memorial service.)

∞

"The love and prayers, the depth of thought and motivation from the heart for dear Gayle that you and others extended to her was momentous, and I know with certainty that Gayle was there and taking part in all of it with gratitude." (This statement was written about Dr. Pierce after her transition, on March 15, 1999, at the age of 95). V. M.

FROM THE AUTHOR

My quest for spiritual knowledge began a long time ago, although it was at first a nameless internal impulse. This impulse was my motivation for participating in numerous workshops, some of which were sponsored by the Creative Growth Center located in Los Gatos, California. This foundation, created by Dorothy Allen, gave me the opportunity to meet many spiritual practitioners, teachers and leaders from diverse cultures and backgrounds. It was during a visit with Dorothy in 1968 that she spoke of someone she wanted me to meet. Without further discussion, she dialed a number and handed me the phone. A voice said, "This is Dr. Pierce." Walking into the unknown, I began my more than thirty-year association with Dr. Pierce as a patient, a student and a friend.

Before meeting Dorothy Allen and Dr. Pierce, I had traveled for five years in the Far, Near, and Middle East. This journey gave me the opportunity to experience Eastern cultures as well as their traditions, and to study Hinduism, Buddhism, and Islam. This strange and unfamiliar cultural exposure changed my perspective of life. I became aware that I was seeking spiritual truths as well as a personal experience of them. My background as a Roman Catholic sheltered me at the time of my travels from altering my beliefs; however, a few years after my return to the United States I knew with certainty that there was a limitation for me within the framework of an organized religion—I had to seek elsewhere. My faith in God remained steadfast, although the platform of my beliefs was shattered.

Because of my prior participation in seminars, my travels, and an expanded awareness that I frequently experienced in Dr. Pierce's presence, I believed I understood the teachings she conveyed, but it wasn't always so.

Gayle was an intense listener and a person of few words except in spiritual matters. Her words frequently reverberated in my mind for days and impelled me to develop new patterns of thought. I found the teachings interesting, stimulating and absorbing. I became inquisitive, and with that curiosity came a seemingly endless number of questions to which she sometimes responded. By not answering all of my questions, Gayle encouraged me to develop the gifts of discernment and discrimination which became the foundation for my spiritual path, and my commitment to it.

For many years, I traveled weekly from San Francisco to San Jose to stay overnight at Dr. Pierce's residence which became my second home. For two summers I lived with her and received cranial therapy from her skilled hands. This intense and often painful form of therapy frequently exposed stored emotions.

Since Gayle arose early, there were many mornings when I awoke to the whirl of the blender. When I came downstairs later I would find her in the kitchen mixing a pineapple protein drink with fresh mint from her garden. This was our breakfast. Then it was time for prayer. Often there were other house guests, and we would sit as a group for healing and for meditation.

Gayle had a solid grasp of world affairs, a unique and creative sense of arrangement, a love of travel, and exceptional culinary skills. She was loyal and protective of those she loved. I remember her waving good-bye as I drove back to San Francisco where I worked initially as a teacher, and later as a social worker and psychotherapist.

Even though she always said she was not a teacher, for more than twenty-five years I trained and studied healing and spiritual practices under Dr. Pierce's guidance, both to help others as well as myself.

My friendship with Gayle was warm and stabilizing. She supported, encouraged, and challenged almost every aspect of my life. Her spoken word was never superficial. She continually strove to teach me to honor my intuition and my growth, to be purposeful in my spiritual search, to be pure of thought, to have faith in myself, and to develop the inherent and latent gifts that I was born with in this lifetime.

In the evenings, we enjoyed PBS (Public Broadcasting Station). While she rested on a small sofa covered by a colorful crocheted shawl, I curled up on a small settee—one or both of us asleep at times. The growth of our friendship was close to my heart. It was a time of comradeship. I especially remember the laughter. These moments, these times, for me, were years of growth, confrontation, striving, joy, change, shedding of concepts, and the sharing of stories, values, and experiences.

Occasionally we shopped for food, infrequently attended concerts and sometimes dined out. In 1976, we took a lengthy trip to Romania, Turkey, and Bulgaria. We stayed in the Carpathian Mountains and on the Baltic Sea coast. Daily prayer and meditation enhanced this trip which was both a great highlight and spiritual pilgrimage. During that time, we contacted and worked with the Masters who reside in the Carpathian Mountains. Our health improved, and each of us experienced many spiritual blessings.

Growth on the Path is about the spiritual journey. Without you, Gayle, this book would not be nor would I be who I am. So it is with grateful thanks that I continue on my way, and it is my desire that those who read this book may find support for themselves on their path.

AGNI YOGA BOOK LIST

Numerous books were studied in the Agni Yoga groups and the meditation groups. Those personally favored by Dr. Pierce are followed by an asterisk (*).

SERIES (books by Helena Roerich)

*Leaves of Morya's Garden Vol.I (The Call)**
Leaves of Morya's Garden Vol. II (Illumination)
New Era Community
Agni Yoga
*Infinity 1**
*Infinity 2**
*Hierarchy**
*Fiery World I**
Fiery World II
Fiery World III
Brotherhood

*Letters of Helena Roerich, Vol I**
*Letters of Helena Roerich, Vol II**
Foundations of Buddhism

BOOKLETS (compiled from books of the Agni Yoga series)

Mother of the World

Mother of Agni Yoga

Woman

A Treasury of Terms and Thoughts from the Agni Yoga Teachings

The Roerich Pact and the Banner of Peace

BOOKS (by Nicholas Roerich)

Altai-Himalaya, A Travel Diary

The Invincible

Shambhala

Heart of Asia

VIDEO

Nicholas Roerich, Messenger of Beauty, Video cassette, 45 minutes, NTSC, or PAL. Contains 160 paintings, music, commentary about Roerich, readings from his poetry.

All books listed under Agni Yoga are obtainable from the Nicholas Roerich Museum, 319 West 107th Street, New York, NY 10025-2799.

Agni Yoga Book List

These books are also available online at www.roerich.org

tel-212/864-7752

fax-212/864-7704

e-mail: orders@roerich.org

OTHER BOOKS

Nicholas Roerich, A Biography, by Garabed Paelian

Nicholas Roerich, Life and Art of a Russian Master, * by Jacqueline Decter (eighty-eight color plates, a full biography, and documentary photographs)

Messenger of Beauty: The Life and Visionary Art of Nicholas Roerich by Jacqueline Decter, Park Street Press; Reprint edition (November 1, 1997)

Nicholas Roerich, by Kenneth Archer (one hundred paintings, with extensive commentaries on thirty-two of the paintings)

When the Sun Moves Northward, * by Mabel Collins, published by Theosophical Publishing House, Ltd.

Sacred Symbols of the Ancients — With Supplements of Yearly Progressions and Birth Card Cycle-Graphs, * by Edith L. Randall and Florence Evylinn Campbell, M.A., published by DeVorss & Company, Marina del Rey, California, 1947, 1974, 1989

Ogamisama Says..., published by Tensho-Kotai-Jingu-Kyo, Tabuse, Yamaguchi Pref., Japan

Psychological Commentaries on the teaching of Gurdjieff and Ouspensky, * Vols.1-5 by Maurice Nicoll. 1949-1952, reprinted 1996 by Atrium Publishers Group

A Vision of India: The Art of Elizabeth Sass Brunner and Elizabeth Brunner, * Introduction by Jaya Appasamy and published by Allied Publishers Private Limited, New York, 1979

Light on the Path, * by Mabel Collins, published by Yogi Publication Society

The Mahatma Letters, * Rider and Company, New York

BOOKS BY MARIE CORELLI

The Distant Voice: A Fact or Fancy

A Romance of Two Worlds

The Secret Power

Vendetta! The Story of One Forgotten

The Young Diana: An Experiment of the Future

Ziska: The Problem of a Wicked Soul

ISBN 1412066616-6